Blessed Are You

Also by Mother Mary Francis, P.C.C.

A Right to Be Merry
Anima Christi
A Time of Renewal
Cause of Our Joy
Strange Gods Before Me
But I Have Called You Friends
Forth and Abroad
Where Caius Is
Summon Spirit's Cry
La Madre
Counted as Mine

For more titles, please visit
www.poorclares-roswell.org
or write to:
Poor Claire Monastery of Our Lady of Guadalupe
809 East Nineteenth Street
Roswell, NM 88201

Mother Mary Francis, P.C.C.

Blessed Are You
Reflections on the Beatitudes

SOPHIA INSTITUTE PRESS
Manchester, New Hampshire

Cover design by LUCAS Art & Design, Jenison, MI.

On the cover: green leaves, courtesy of Unsplash; watercolor leaves
and branches courtesy of CreativeMarket.

Scripture quotations are taken from the Douay Rheims version of the Bible.

Sophia Institute Press
Box 5284, Manchester, NH 03108
1-800-888-9344

www.SophiaInstitute.com

Sophia Institute Press® is a registered trademark of Sophia Institute.

paperback ISBN 978-1-64413-424-5

ebook ISBN 978-1-64413-425-2

Library of Congress Control Number: 2021936385

First printing

To
His Eminence,
Augustine Cardinal Mayer, O.S.B.,
blessed champion of religious life

Contents

Preface

Others have written of the Beatitudes. No one, however, with such compelling insight as Mother Mary Francis of the Poor Clare Monastery in Roswell, New Mexico. She approaches these as a whole, interdependent, complementary, one interpreting the other and illumining its apparent obscurity. Mother Francis savors their spirit of Beatitude and witnesses to the gift of bliss and happiness that they offer to those who listen and reflect. But she shares with her readers her sharp-eyed awareness of the cost of this Beatitude that is "not as the world gives." An outstanding instance would be her definition of why to mourn is to enjoy a wondrous grace, for to mourn is to give "the right response to penancing truth." Only a poet could have the tender hardiness to choose that adjective "penancing"—and only a heart of spiritual depth could decipher the joy, not only of the angels in Heaven, but also of the sinner who does the penance the truth discloses. Mother Francis has written much and well, unafraid to sing of the blessedness of those who hear the word of God and keep it.

But, one feels, in this slim book she has exhibited an originality and a loving-kindness which marks her off as singularly open and sensitive to the yearnings of today. Yes, to live the Beatitudes is to create that inner space wherein there is no limit to what the Spirit of God can do to the generous soul. A costly operation for us, for the pearl of great price is not bought cheap. But "O the bliss" of the vision which these pages reveal, and how tawdry the limping spiritual direction of those who advocate a man-made programme of discipleship.

May God be honored and praised by the work of His servant, a true Poor Clare whose only sorrow is that so many have not yet found the way to eternal life by lives grounded in the bliss of the Beatitudes.

—Alan C. Clark
Bishop of Elmham
Chairman (appointed by Pope St. Paul VI)
of the Anglican/Roman Catholic
International Ecumenical Commission
Poringland, Norwich,
Norfolk, England

Blessed Are You

Blessed are the poor in spirit:
for theirs is the kingdom of Heaven

It was all so simple. Jesus climbed up a hill and sat down there on the grassy slope. And, looking around Him and down before Him at all those eager upturned faces, He spoke as no man had ever spoken before. Yes, with authority, as Matthew was to comment on the occasion of the Evangelical discourse (Matt. 7:29). But also with heartbreaking simplicity. We have tended to associate heartbreak with pain and sadness. Yet we know that there are many sword-thrusts that break the heart. Joy. A flash of sheer understanding. The burning simplicity of truth stripped of cumbersome trappings of words and shining like a rapier in the sun. All of these break up the hard clods of the heart and make it new.

3

Christ was about to deliver the Christian philosophy of life and give the first course in theological living. And He delivered it and He gave it in words so simple that all through the centuries the exegetes have been trying to explain them to us, sometimes to our help and sometimes to our hindrance. We make best use of the help and free ourselves of the hindrance by immersing ourselves, each one in prayer and reflection, on the message itself, so limited verbally and so utterly pure. "*Candor est lucis aeternae!*" One must already have attained, by preservation or by reparation, to some measure of the sixth Beatitude to be prepared for the message of any of the Beatitudes. Blessed are the clean of heart; they shall see God. Blessed are the clean of heart; they alone hear God and heed Him. One must be without guile.

In the motley group that Christ addressed, there were many different personalities, many different backgrounds, many different sets-of-heart. Many of the poor were certainly in that crowd, the materially poor. And some of the rich, some of the Pharisees and Scribes, some of them honestly looking for the truth, some of them there out of curiosity, some of them there to try to catch Him in His speech. Each would hear, according to his capacity to hear. Those without guile of heart would hear truth and espouse

4

it. Those with guileful hearts would hear truth and disclaim it. Any who were trying to trap Christ in His speech, to find something untenable in what He said, would assuredly have the dark reward of finding what they were looking for. One is always able to turn the world of divine truth to one's own ruin if one wishes. So with the curious. They would find something diverting, but certainly not to be taken seriously. One remembers Herod.

There were the others, though, who sat on the grass wanting only to hear what He would have to say, and to hear it with a willing and open heart, not in an argumentative frame of mind, not even in a dialogic reference of mind, but only to listen and to be made aware of their greatness and to be healed of whatever infirmities of thought they had had before. We want to align ourselves with them.

When He spoke to this great crowd of people, Jesus said, first of all: "Blessed are the poor in spirit: for theirs is the kingdom of Heaven." Here was the simple presentation of His plan for holiness, for the true revolutionizing of the world and of souls. One wants to suck at the meaning as earnestly as a baby nursing at its mother's breast, to suck at every word that fell from those blessed lips. So, first of all, what does "blessed" mean?

We know, with all respect for certain translations, that it does not mean just "happy." Rather, it signifies being favored, set apart, already hallowed, holy. Literally, it denotes that sealed-for-holiness of which the young nun sings at her first profession. "He has set a mark upon me." That is what the blessed ones are: those with the mark of God upon them, those set apart, those bearing a seal, the hallowed ones, the favored ones. And Christ said that this is the condition of those who are poor in spirit. Surely one would like to reflect on some of the qualities of those in so blessed a condition that Jesus does not just promise them a future reward but guarantees a present one. Blessed are the meek, the gentle; they shall inherit the earth. Blessed are they who mourn; they shall be comforted. These things shall come about. But only to the poor in spirit and to those suffering for His name's sake does the Savior speak of immediacy in describing the consequence. Again, those who make peace shall be known as the children of God in eternity. Perhaps even on earth they shall one day be recognized as meriting that title. And blessed are the pure; they shall one day be given the ability to see God. But blessed are the poor. Theirs is the kingdom of God. It is not a promise for the future but a present reward.

In considering the qualities of these blessed poor ones in spirit who already own Heaven, we can gather them into the generic fold of contentedness before we reflect on them specifically. It is an all-pervasive serenity of soul that marks the truly poor in spirit. Contentedness, but very active contentedness. The contentedness of those who have penetrated the meaning of *fiat!* Those who have gathered strength out of suffering to pronounce upon the fabric itself as well as upon the pattern and the detail of their lives, the simple, dignified, noble: "Let it be!" The poor in spirit are not restive, not squirmingly intent upon alterations of present reality, but able to isolate the ultimate Reality in the present details. They are in charge of their will, which is indeed free under their steering. They are not ground down by people, by situations, by circumstances, however much they may suffer from them. Rather, they are flexible to all of these. And that may be the first quality of the poor in spirit.

How graceful an expression of contentedness is flexibility! It is to be rooted only in God. Not in circumstances, in situations, in persons, nor, above all, in oneself, in one's own desires. It belongs to that docility that is the quality of being teachable. There is an old Swedish proverb that is very meaningful in this regard. When I heard a Swedish

7

friend first articulate it, I could not quite make out what she was saying for her heavy accent. She was telling how her mother had always told her, "*Der bush das der best ben.*" At least, that is how it sounded to my dull ear. A space of pondering and a slower repetition yielded the meaning: "The bush that is the best, bends." And so with persons.

He who is poor in spirit bends most easily to God's inspirations, is the least susceptible of confusing God's inspirations with his own plans and desires. The inflexible person is very susceptible of such confusion. And inflexibility of spirit can show itself in surprising ways if we seriously ponder poverty of spirit and the lack of it. There is, for example, the great delusion of preferring to sanctify ourselves rather than to allow ourselves to be sanctified by God. It is the Holy Spirit who sanctifies us, and efforts to achieve the effects of His divine ministry by our own blueprints and constructions will always be unavailing, however enticing. We do not learn very quickly here. Nor does continued failure appear to daunt us in our endeavors to arrogate the ministry of the Holy Spirit to ourselves.

But then there may arise the small, nagging question: "Are we not masters of our own fate? Is not choice ours? How do we reconcile abandonment — flexible, graceful, beautiful surrender—with self-determination?" It is not, after all, such a conundrum as it would like to appear.

Really, it is the same thought gone all the way around to meet itself and find itself the same. For, yes, it is our choice and our choices in life to make; and, yes, we are masters of our fate. We can choose whether God shall sanctify us or whether we shall exhaust ourselves and waste our lives in our own self-directed "sanctification." This is a tremendous freedom. That freedom of the best bush—the one that bends.

It is a bitter, constricting, withering thing to claim Godship for ourselves. This is the oldest sin, to "be like God," to achieve our own sanctification not by seeking after God's desires and the unfolding of His will, but in the achievement of what we have decided is our sanctification. In this, the wisest man in the world is an utter dullard, for not one of us knows the mystery of our sanctification. We have only the terrible freedom of allowing ourselves to be sanctified by God—or of refusing.

Flexibility in accepting and espousing God's plan for our sanctity is one of the most subtle of all detachments, one of the most precious of all riches, and maybe the one we are least ready to claim. The dubious currency that buys sanctification by manipulation of reality can rub so well between one's fingers. How often the saints have been sanctified in their acceptance of God's plans, which were the seeming frustration of their own. Few of them have been notably marked with success as the world appraises success. What success really means is in the secret of God's Face. Whether a thing comes off grandiosely or even passingly well does not really matter. We are called to be seekers—alert, ready, flexible to respond. How things turn out is God's business. How we do them and how we respond to them is our business. Flexibility is so very characteristic of those who are poor in spirit.

One sees what happens to the inflexible growth in the storm. It is the unbending tree that falls, the uncurving stalks that are broken. The bending grasses remain; the flowers can defy a tornado with their arabesques. Spiritual flexibility allows us to be disposable, disponible before God. And, far from being equated with passivity, it demands action, arduous and persevering action. The ballerina does not achieve flexibility without long practice and much travail. Still less does the dancer in spirit arrive at sheer grace without effort. Is this not what the poor in spirit are—the dancers of the Lord? Bending in adversity, on pointe in the sun, liftable, lightsome, full of movement because unencumbered.

The bush that is the best, bends; it has life. The poor in spirit have their foundations only in God and have understood that "We have not here a lasting city" (Heb. 13:14). They bend. They move. They are flexible. They are free and full of song because they have already the kingdom of Heaven for their earthly dwelling place.

And then there is vulnerability. To be poor in spirit and possess the kingdom of Heaven, one must agree to be vulnerable. Those who are truly poor in spirit must deliver over to others the power to hurt them, for without this there is no loving. And without love, we can have only a masque of being poor-in-spirit, that masque of pride and complacency under which one feeds on one's supposed successes in poverty and is sadly protected from real understanding. There are various expressions of the vulnerability proper to the poor in spirit. One has to let disjointed members be straightened. And this will never be accomplished without pain. One has to let oneself be exploited and misunderstood, for this belongs to loving. Our blessed Lord in His earthly life showed Himself very vulnerable.

Christ wanted to be loved; He wanted helpers; He wanted friends. When they slept in His hour of need, He rebuked them: "Could you not watch one hour with me?"

(Matt. 26:40). He wanted His friends to be with Him. And when He gave gifts, when He cured ten and was thanked by only one, He revealed to us His suffering human heart: "Where are the nine?" (Luke 17:17). He wanted love and wanted gratitude. He desired those things that any normal human heart desires. The Son of God was poor in spirit. He was vulnerable, and He was willing to go on being vulnerable after He had been hurt. We do not find Jesus saying the equivalent of, "Well, that is that! That is the last time I shall ever do anything for lepers. What is the use? Why scatter gifts to people who do not even thank me for them?" Nor did He revoke the cure for the ungrateful nine.

Our Savior did not ever strive to arm Himself with invulnerability when He was wounded, but He showed Himself willing to go on being hurt even unto His Passion and death and post-death piercing. He went on working with the sorry little lot of humanity in which we find ourselves and which made up the chorus of His earthly life. He kept His vulnerability unstained. He kept His vulnerability pure. And for us who want to stumble after Him, it is necessary that we never refuse to give more when gratitude has been withheld, that we never refuse to go on loving because our love has been betrayed. What of the tragedy of the Apostolic College? For Him, it was not a matter of concluding, as it might well be for us: "Well, this is the end! I cannot have even twelve men without one of them betraying me. What is the use?" He went on, the poor and suffering Servant. And in the end, He managed to make eleven into the Church because He was willing to be vulnerable to men's assaults on His love, to men's betrayals, to men's denials, to men's persevering failures. His love survived all these, triumphed over them, was willing to be wounded again and again, never descended to inaction when rejected, never came to a halt when His best efforts seemed to come to nothing, not even when they were flung back in His divine Face. The flexible, the poor in spirit, likewise bend under blows and adversities of the spirit. They are willing to remain vulnerable. And that is why they are poor in spirit.

If we want to check on our own Christlike vulnerability in poverty of spirit, perhaps our surest check will be found in our unwillingness to hurt another. The vulnerable ones are those most solicitous that others should not be wounded. Without subscribing to spiritual stocktaking, we can well afford to conduct this brief investigation about ourselves.

The flexibility and vulnerability characteristic of the poor in spirit make possible that freedom which is their hallmark. The poor in spirit are, in point of fact, the only ones who are truly free. They are not locked up in a little cage of self so that when they attempt to fly, all they can do is hurt their wings. The really poor in spirit are the adventuresome people. These are the ones who, like St. Francis and St. Clare, always delight and exhilarate in the wonder of life, however suffering some aspects of life may be. No more than Francis or Clare do any of the poor in spirit go about with a sullen face because God's blueprints of the day are found constrictive. They go about radiant with the adventuresomeness of things. We never know what surprises God has planned. Not one of us knows what the day holds, what God has designed for our sanctification, what ambitions God has for our growth in holiness today. And so we can live with a tingling sense of adventuresomeness if we are free with the freedom of the children of God, those who are really poor in spirit, who do not dwell in cages of self, but can fly free. Even in a very small space, they enjoy the kingdom of Heaven.

The poor in spirit greet the day with wonder, expecting surprises if only and precisely because they come from God, and perhaps especially so when that alone gives reason for any delight. The inflexible, those who desire invulnerability, are made sullen by surprises. If we approach the day as persons truly poor in spirit, alive with a sense of anticipation — "What does the day hold?" — we also begin to experience something of a divine sense of humor. We get glimmers of understanding that, in truth, God's ways are not our ways nor His thoughts our thoughts; but that as far as the heavens are above the earth, so God's thoughts are above the thoughts of men (Isa. 55:8–9). It is a profound scriptural declaration, yes, and appropriately solemn. Yet is it not also replete with humor? Is it not really a delicious saying? I sometimes wonder whether the inspired writer did not have a genially wry smile on his face as he set down those words.

If we could be this free, if we could have this sense of being surprised, if we understood that the things that take us off guard and upset our plans, whether work plans or grandiose plans for our own sanctification, are delightful "alerts" from God, how joyously we could live! Are these things not God saying very intimately: "Look, you have got the whole thing wrong! My thoughts are not your thoughts." The poor in spirit are those who have learned to greet the unexpected with a sense of humble humor, of good-natured humility. One can turn this about either way, for a sense of humor is never far removed from a sense of light. A sense of humor is also as far removed from anything

15

that is sullen, anything that is self-pitying, anything that is grudging, as the heavens are from the earth. Flexible, vulnerable, the poor in spirit are free. Not landowners, not plan-owners, they have already come into the estate of the kingdom of Heaven.

Directly out of that quality, atmosphere, reality of freedom which is the third characteristic of the poor in spirit as we run down our observations, is the fourth quality of being without holdings. It is so significant that, in that all-embracing prayer that is the sequence for the Mass of Pentecost, the Holy Spirit has us cry out: "Come, Father of the Poor!" and then add: "Bring all your gifts along. Come, Giver of gifts." The poor ones are supposed to be the expectant ones. The truly poor in spirit are prepared for receptivity. They are vibrantly receptive to all that God gives, whether spiritual, material, emotional, psychological. There is no artificiality here, no self-conscious "detachment." Only those without holdings can be really receptive. Landowners and plan-owners in the realm of the spirit will be merely acquisitive.

What could it mean on the material plane: to be unartificial, to be without holdings? Does it not imply that we shall neither despise nor undervalue on the one hand, or on the other hand exhibit and experience complacency

in the external forms of poverty? Artificiality has many
expressions, and the more dangerous ones can look surprisingly like holiness. Our poverty certainly does not primarily
consist in foregoing fine garments and dainty foods. Nor
do I think there is the hardy stuff of "temptations" in these
for most of us. At least, I know of no one who is suffering
from the lack of silk lingerie or who is troubled about the
dress pattern we have not changed for hundreds of years.
Yet we cannot be so foolish as to suppose that materialities
do not matter. They do matter, if they are expressions of
the interior. They are a falsification if they are attempting
to substitute for attitudinal poverty of the spirit.

It is a normal reaction, perhaps we could even say a
healthy reaction, that we do not always care for the food
that is served. It could sometimes be tempting to want a
more comfortable bed. But these things are scarcely material for anguish. It would be too bad to make them into
material for self-satisfaction. For there is an artificiality
that can be proud of its patches. There is a superficiality of
spirit by which we can try to establish a security in material
expressions of poverty. To be sure, it would be preposterous
to think we need have no care for the material expressions.
And this kind of nonsense is being set forth by entirely too
many spiritual draft-dodgers these days. It is ridiculous to

think that we could make a boudoir out of our cell or make a lounge-type recreation center out of our community room, concluding that these things do not matter because we are all poor in spirit. Or that we could scatter comfortable deck chairs over the lawns for leaning back and expatiating on poverty of spirit. No, these things are meaningful. But they have to spring out of a much deeper thing, and they themselves are not the things on which we establish our poverty. While exercising vigilance to maintain a material sparseness and leanness and simplicity, we also want to fear the smugness that boasts, even if only in the auditorium of the mind: "I sleep on a hard, narrow bed. I sit on a backless bench. I eat boiled potatoes and canned beets. I am poor." True poverty of spirit is both attitudinal and material. The latter has meaning only because of the former. The poor in spirit are without holdings of any kind. Even those holdings that are ownership of the pride of being without holdings.

If we look for a fifth characteristic of the poor in spirit, we shall surely note: creativity. Prerequisites for the contemplative life have been set down by Andrée Emery[1] as

[1] Andrée Emery, Ph.D., member of the Secular Institute of Our Lady of the Way, staff member of Hacker Psychiatric Clinic, Los Angeles, California.

(1) a high degree of creativity, and (2) a capacity for the humdrum. This seems to me very insightful, but I would hesitate at the "and." Surely there can be and ought to be a great degree of creativity in the humdrum of every day. This is what the poor in spirit discover and manifest. Those who cannot make creative the so-called humdrum things of daily living are scarcely creative persons. They are not poor in spirit, not possessed of that flexibility and elected vulnerability that are essential to creativity, not established in that freedom and that state of being without holdings that give creativity full scope.

We have a telling example in the life of St. Jane Frances de Chantal. Aristocrat that she was, it is likely that she had her first experience with sweeping up dust after she entered the convent. One day Jane Frances was gathering in the dust with utmost care, and another sister was watching her. "It is only dust," commented the watcher who seems to have been not very notable for a sense of wonder. "You act as though you were sweeping up pearls."

This was altogether too much care and creativity for dust. But St. Jane Frances smiled: "Pearls? Oh, better than pearls. It is the dust of the house of God." This was a woman of insight and creativity rather beyond that of her observer.

For the truly creative person, there is no humdrum. The kind of creativeness of heart that the saint was able to manifest when sweeping up dust belongs to the poor in spirit. Loving to beautify the little that we have is a deep part of poverty of spirit. It is not that we want dinginess. It is not that we are satisfied with dreariness. It is that we are creative enough to wrest beauty out of places and things where it may not seem to exist. We can be glad that we live here in a desert land — not just settled down in lush countryside to be enjoyed but obliged to be always busy about trying to work with God in wresting beauty out of places where beauty has not of itself appeared. And so it is in all works. The truly poor ones add to their situation always the high creativity of trying to beautify what they have, however little it may seem to be.

Lightness and gaiety belong to attitudinal poverty, not merely imposed poverty. Bleakness must never be confused with poverty, nor should dinginess or even starkness be identified with it. St. Francis did not talk of poverty, but of holy poverty, and especially of his Lady Poverty. She was to him a beautiful ideal, and he sought out his little hermitages in places of beauty that he beautified all the more. He adorned his own austerity, just as St. Clare beautified hers. The poor work with what is given them. And this does not by any means exclude the gifts of the rich.

If a gift is poor and lowly per se, the creative poor in spirit receive it with humility. But they do not set aside with hauteur what is per se less poor and less lowly. The rich, too, must be allowed to love and to give. And their gifts are to be shared and diffused.

Flexible to the whole life situation, bending to God and to fellow men, loving devotedly on and on in the vulnerability of the poor Christ, free and spiritually nomadic, pitching what tents God indicates and where He points out, the poor in spirit exercise always that creativity that is their heritage from the Father. And out of all these qualities is formed that capacity for enjoyment, delight, wonder, which is so eminently characteristic of the poor in spirit. *Il Poverello* found two sticks by the roadside. "A violin!" Madman or little poor one of the Lord according to one's perspective, insight, and frame of reference, St. Francis played his "violin" in praise of the Most High God. "I am the herald of the Great King," he announced, though there were undoubtedly some who thought he was not dressed for the part.

It is definitely not a property of austerity to be closed to delight. This would be to revert to what we reflected on earlier: putting down our holdings. The poor cannot put down holdings, not even in austerity. They are called to be open to the Lord, responsive to whatever He gives. If He gives lightness of spirit, if He gives an emotional upsurge — thanks be to Him. If He gives a headache or a heartache — thanks be to Him. Poor in spirit, receiving with open hands and open heart whatever God gives directly or through others, we become little enough to understand that this receiving whatever is given is part of that attitudinal poorness that is poverty of spirit. On the material plane, if it is the gift of fish so full of bones, we can exercise delicate artistry in removing them. On the spiritual plane, we exercise the same grace in accepting God's ways of sanctifying us in the situations of the day. And that brings us right back to our initial characteristic of the poor in spirit: flexibility.

If we are loaded up like a safety deposit box with the blueprints for our own sanctification, the deeds for our holdings, the folio of our austerity, the armor against hurt, there is scarcely going to be room in us for the Holy Spirit and His gifts. For they are not few. It would be altogether too bad to have stocked our own receptivity when the Giver of all good gifts is looking for the poor in spirit to enrich them. If we are overflowing with our own ideas, we cannot be open to His. Neither can He give us His light (*Veni, Lumen cordium*) if our hearts are shaded with our own plans, our own decisions, judgments, verdicts. Certainly, we use our own powers of decision-making, evaluating, concluding. But in the employment of them, we remain so flexible, teachable, open to the Lord, that we do not confuse our own voice with God's. We all have turning points in our lives, those we presently recognize as major and those that we perhaps see only in retrospect as determinative. Each day is, in fact, a turning point. However, there come great turning points when we make particular choices that may revolve about what seems of itself a very little thing. And by these choices the caliber of our lives is substantiated. You know John Bunker's poem in which he describes his friend who made the wrong small choice, took the wrong slight turning. "A different path, one way instead of another — merely took what seemed to him the way of easier treading." And the poet goes on to detail how "by the strange irony of the unforeseen, the path he chose became for him indeed the difficult way of pain and loneliness that leads to God knows whither."[2] This day, too, will be replete with choices for us to make, choices

---

[2] John Bunker, "Dark Fields and Shining Towers."

for coming closer to God as the little poor ones intent upon expressing His will, eager to give Him delight with the dancing of their flexible spirits before His face. John Bunker's friend merely took what seemed to him a better choice for self. As such choices often enough do, that one led him in the end down a difficult path indeed.

For the poor in spirit, the vulnerable, the receptive, the free, the creative, the way of their flexible choices leads, in an entirely different sense, to God knows whither. Yes, God knows whither. And it is not necessary that we should know where. It is only necessary that we be poor enough to respond readily and follow eagerly.

Blessed are the meek:
for they shall possess the land

Christ went on to tell His doubtless spellbound listeners about a large legacy and who was to receive it. Some people were to inherit the land, to possess the earth. Their identification must certainly have been startling to that large congregation on the hillside. Meekness then, even as now, was not generally considered to be the outstanding mark of large landowners. Yet that was what He said. "Blessed are the meek: for they shall possess the land" (Matt. 5:4).

Our chaplain, Father Burcard Fischer, O.F.M., once remarked in a homily and with quite some acuity that the first land the meek possess is the land they are standing on. They are whole persons. They take that firm stance that only the gentle can really assume. The domineering, the aggressive, the blustering are not so much taking a stance as posturing. What we shall want first to consider in the meek, then, is their strength.

The meek are the self-possessed, which is to say that they are God-possessed since God has been allowed to possess their "selves." The arrogant and aggressive have leased their "selves" out to their acquisitiveness, their ambition, their desire to domineer. And while it is a poor enough bargain, they seem to go on renewing the lease for the meager return, the even self-destructive return. They never really possess the land on which they stand; they merely wage war over it.

If meekness is not exactly the worldly ideal, neither is it universally correlated with strength. Contrariwise, is not the first connotation of meekness in many minds that of supineness, spiritlessness, weakness? It is strange that this should be so, when Jesus set forth meekness as the expression of His own divine-human heart. It is interesting that Christ asked us to master only one lesson plan in life: "Learn of me, because I am meek, and humble of heart" (Matt. 11:29). It is certainly not without significance that He never specifically asked us to learn anything else. He knew the hearts of men and what was in them then, what is in them now. He understood that excellence in humility and meekness requires the practiced ease possible only to a whole lifetime of striving. A doctorate in meekness requires a studious dedication that not too many are prepared to make.

We remember that our blessed Lord also spoke of taking on a yoke. "Take my yoke upon you, and learn of me, because I am meek, and humble of heart" (Matt. 11:29). Meekness is the very opposite of irresponsibility. Rather, in opting for emulation of the meek Christ, we are agreeing to take on a highly demanding responsibility. But there is this about the heaviest responsibilities: they are never oppressive. It can be, after all, highly exhilarating to lift something heavy and carry it. It requires much practice and dogged determination, but among the rewards are the experience of spiritual élan in oneself and the presentation of a beautiful example to others.

When the danseur lifts the ballerina high into the air and seems to float her about over his head, it is not because obscure gravitational statistics of the dance reveal that one hundred and ten pounds become ten pounds when delivered from earthly moorings. No, rather the danseur has learned how to lift a one-hundred-pounds-plus burden that is sweet to him. The weight has become a part of the beauty he is creatively expressing. He is for us a model of bearing heavy responsibility, quite literally, with ease and grace. He has had to learn how to do this. The danseur has been obliged to try and to experience failure and then to try again and again and again. The weight of responsibility borne with practiced grace has been transformed into the lightness of achievement. But one has to bear the burden, to carry it, to lift it, to sweep it up. It will always be nothing but oppressive when pulled or dragged along.

Jesus again invites us to respond to his initiative with our own. It is His yoke, this humility, this meekness. But we are to take it up. He does not yoke it upon us but suggests that we yoke it upon ourselves. His yoke becomes our elected own. "Take my yoke upon you." There must be the labor of learning to lift the burden before we can discover the burden light. Excellence in meekness is not for the lethargic, the apathetic, the ungenerous. But it is more than élan that our blessed Savior promises us for becoming practiced in His meekness. He talks of rest: "And you shall find rest for your souls."

Reposefulness is an outstanding characteristic of the meek. And it is more the magnificent reposefulness of the mountain, firm and strong and equal to the blast of adverse winds, than of the sleeper. One could agree that the meek possess the land they are standing on and go on to add that they possess themselves. The Beatitudes were not departmentalized by Christ. One flows into another. The next is possible because of the others. One expression leads to another. Each in a sense explains all the others. And so that quality (and not only state) of being without holdings, the characteristic of the poor in spirit, is clearly illustrated by the meek.

Because they are without holdings, the meek actually hold everything. We see this patently in the life of St. Francis. The poet's fancy of "swinging the earth a trinket at my wrist"[3] became spiritual reality in the little Poor Man of Assisi. That all the earth was his is apparent in the way Francis dealt with the earth. He communed with it, eulogized it, singing expressions of its Creator, was literally familial with it. There was never a man more at home in creation than meek Francis of Assisi. To the pilgrim alone belongs the land, for the pilgrim is only happily passing through. He is not about to declare wars of colonization. He does not in fact need colonies. He has it all.

Thus there is this reposefulness about the meek. Without aggressiveness (he suffers no grinding to possess),

[3] Francis Thompson, "The Hound of Heaven."

without arrogance (for he is a son and heir of a Master whose infinite holdings are never in jeopardy and who assigns meekness as birthright to His progeny), he is at rest. The world is so torn with aggression, so swollen with arrogance. For this acute restiveness and for this diseasedness there is no repose. Rather than submit to this prognosis, we often enough pretend to despise re-posefulness. Life is for action, protest, apprehension! But we shall want to reflect a bit later that the hunger and thirst for justice that signals yet another Beatitude calls for an action, a protest, and an apprehension possible only to the meek.

Flailing one's arms about becomes in the end merely exhausting, and that kind of exhaustion makes repose impossible. Insisting on one's rights, suing for them with merciless domination, fills the air with noise but never with music. Music belongs to the meek who have the strength to suffer all things patiently for the love of Christ and, in the end to "count them but as dung, that I may gain Christ" (Phil. 3:8).

"You shall find rest to your souls" (Matt. 11:29). The strength of the meek, the strength that is able to suffer and to suffer gladly, is identified in reposefulness. And in this reposefulness one can experience what it is to possess the land. Only those who do not stake out particular holdings are free enough to possess all of the earth. The meek have learned to possess their own souls in peace. Therefore they stand without fear upon the land become theirs not by acquisition but by gift and reward. And they become free to roam the whole territory of their inheritance: the earth.

So it was that Jesus said: Blessed are the meek; they shall own everything. They shall possess the whole land. They indeed possess everything who do not stake out any holdings. We need, however, to ask how often and how obstinately we deliver ourselves up to acquisitiveness. We want to own some ideas and judgments and to stake out claims on them. This is my sovereign opinion, which no one shall alter! Certainly, we have basic convictions, but this does not entail succumbing to the aggressiveness of "This is *my* charge, this is *my* work; keep out, keep off the grass of *my* holdings." This idea that is my "holding" is often enough the mistaken idea on which no one is going to correct me. I put up signs and observe squatters' rights. What a dreary business, when we can run and own the land and possess the earth if we are meek and humble of heart!

It is the unending drone of the squatter and his rights that "This is mine. And anyone who wants to liberate me doesn't understand."

There rises the age-old cry: "You don't understand me."
"This is my truth." Or, perhaps more accurately, my veri-
similitude. And no one shall intrude here. No one shall
bring in the truth here. No one shall point to a vision of
something far greater. And so I can sit there and squat
there on my holdings, proud, determined on this ownership, and, of course, forced to defend it. As our Father St.
Francis said, "If we own property, my brothers, then we shall
have to have weapons to defend it."[4] And he went on to
say that this gets more and more complicated. That is just
what happens to us when we stake out a holding. We must
have weapons to defend it. Somebody is coming to say that
I am wrong, but I have weapons to defend my error. And
when we are busily defending this little plot with weapons
of pride, weapons of blindness, weapons of arrogance, we
refuse to possess the land promised to the meek.

Our Lord Jesus Christ has advised us that this is a very
meager way of living. In the end, it is to render life wasted,

---

[4] The Legend of the Three Companions, ch. IX, 33, in St.
Francis of Assisi: Writings and Early Biographies — English
Omnibus of the Sources for the Life of St. Francis, ed. Marion
A. Habig, O.F.M. (Chicago: Franciscan Herald Press,
1972), p. 921.

squandered, lost. He points the direction away from such tragedy. Come to possession of the earth! Possess yourselves in reposefulness of soul. Take up My yoke and stand responsible, yoked, upon firm land. Learn of Me; I am meek and humble of heart. And here is your diploma: the earth.

Blessed are they that mourn:
for they shall be comforted

In a way, that plan for living offered on the Mount of the Beatitudes got stranger as it went along. It might be thought quite enough reversal of worldly philosophy that Christ should have declared that the kingdom belongs to the poor, to have asserted that the whole earth-planet and, by implication, the estates of Heaven as well, are to be given not to the highest bidder or to the most aggressive claimant, but to the serene and reposeful meek. But, no! — there was more to come. For now, into the company of those hallowed by God are brought the weeping ones. "Blessed are they that mourn: for they shall be comforted" (Matt. 5:5).

It is doubtful whether most of us would have arrived unaided at the conclusion that it is a blessed thing to mourn.

If we have any distinct concept of blessedness connected with mourning, it could likely have been that it is a blessed thing to be rid of it. Are not mourners by widely accepted definition the unhappy ones? Obviously, if a mourner is blessed, then it has to mean that he is blessed to have gotten out of this painful predicament, to have escaped from this sorrowful situation, to have fended off suffering. And so we might well have written the third Beatitude like this: Blessed are they who enjoy the comfort of not having anything to mourn about. But then we run up against the hard fact that this is just not what Christ said. Again, His words are not our words. That could have been predicted, since He did mention that His thoughts are not our thoughts (Isa. 55:8). Thoughts at odds with each other are scarcely going to emerge in a verbal identity. We shall have, then, to deal with the words that our blessed Savior uttered and not with the words that we think He ought to have uttered. This confrontation for all its initial difficulty is apt to prove rather more rewarding than we might have supposed. It is, in fact, calculated to revise us, redirect us, reform us, and, in the end, overwhelmingly reward us. What do His words really mean? What, for that matter, do *the* words mean? For we do not ever find Christ manipulating words or re-shaping them to His purpose or showing any predilection for the abstruse. Always, He spoke so simply. This is what devastates us. His words were so plain. That is what is so disconcerting.

It did not matter to Jesus that men even then had tacitly agreed upon a false definition of comfort any more than it matters to Him now. A word is not debauched because we have played it false, even though we may be. And to comfort means "to make strong" (*con* + *fortare*), no matter how much we prattle on about ease and sensual satisfaction. We might, incidentally, pause right there a moment to consider "ease."

To accomplish with ease implies either an initially strong and outstanding gift from God or a previous strong and persevering effort on our own part, and usually both. The poet who writes "with ease" has suffered and labored in order that ease could be possible. The dancer pirouetting with ease has practiced and sweated how many hours? The ease of the concert pianist is the fruit of toilsome years. And even the established ease that comes of persevering effort is never secure of itself but needs always to be sustained by continuing effort. So much for a slight pause to consider ease. Back to comfort.

It is obvious that to make strong is not synonymous with deliverance from difficulty. Rather it already implies just the opposite. We begin here to have an uneasy suspicion that to be comforted, to be made strong, may mean just precisely that we become equipped to bear difficulty. It is a well-founded suspicion. To be comforted in sorrow is to be made strong enough to suffer. If mourning, then, is to be blessed with strength, it cannot of itself be evil. It must, in fact, bear within itself an intrinsic good. How else could God comfort it, much less declare it blessed?

Before we reflect on the radix of mourning, we could stop to recall how we ourselves comfort the mourner. We comfort a sorrowing friend not by removing the cause for sorrow, which is most often quite beyond our power in any case, but by reaching out the strength of our love for our friend, our understanding of his pain, our making ourselves one with him in it. Mother Teresa of Calcutta, heroine of our times, has brought comfort to how many of the wretched dying in India and elsewhere by the strength of her love, by her presence to them? Sometimes we can alleviate certain effects of suffering. We can at times reduce pain with drugs or therapy. Neither of these is actually a comfort, but simply an alleviation, a reduction, a mending. True, physical suffering can sometimes by God-given human skills be ended and pain eventually soothed or even eradicated. But for the mourner, it is a question of the present situation rather than making an end of the situation. There will be finale to mourning, certainly, an eternal soothing, a forever-and-ever eradication. "And God shall wipe away all tears from their eyes: and death shall be no more, nor mourning, nor crying, nor sorrow shall be any more, for the former things are passed away." (Rev. 21:4). But this does not appear to be what Christ is speaking about in the third Beatitude. For He does not talk of the end of mourning, which is to come in life eternal, but of the comforting that is to be given in order that mourning in this life may be possible.

Possible? Yes. For mourning is a very pure thing. Without strength, it degenerates into its very antonym: self-pity. It can even be perverted into bitterness and end in blasphemy. Why does God allow this? Why is God so cruel? Why does God do this to me? How many have sought to punish God by walking no more with Him when He allows them to suffer! "I am through with God. I have had enough of Him." Or "I have stopped going to church. I will show God what He can and cannot do if He expects me to worship Him." Is this our newer mode of making idols? We agree to worship a graven image of our own decisions. We know what is right and what is fitting for God to do. And we shall do homage to a deity who behaves Himself according to the way in which we instruct Him. All this is, of course, to disqualify ourselves for mourning, which is always sprung out of the humility of the creature before the Creator and which is rooted in faith.

But someone may want to raise a small question here. Does not faith of itself cast out mourning? And if I believe that this sorrow, this disappointment, this betrayal is part of a divine plan, would I not show a lack of faith if I mourned over it? It is a good enough question. It has a ready enough answer, even if the answer is part of the whole mystery of suffering.

Why did Christ weep at the tomb of Lazarus? "We have not here a lasting city" (Heb. 13:14). And, "I will raise him up in the last day" (John 6:40). In point of fact, Christ was going to raise Lazarus up that same day and within a very few minutes. And He knew that He was. How explain the tears? A touching demonstration of kinship with the common run of humanity? A lovely bit of play-acting? But Christ never gave demonstrations in the manner of play-acting. "I am ... the truth" (John 14:6). And the truth which He taught at Lazarus's tomb was not only that He has complete power over life and death but also that faith does not eliminate mourning, not even for the Son of God. What is mourning, anyway? There are many kinds of it and many definitions of it: to grieve, to lament, to sorrow, to weep. I would like to propose an addition to the dictionary definitions: to mourn is to make the right response to penancing truth.

Returning to Lazarus, we see that this is exactly what Christ did at the tomb of His friend. Death is a truth. It is right. We have all sinned in Adam and we bear together the penalty. Having come to glorious life out of the dust of nonbeing, we have with Adam obscured the glory. We are redeemed by the Son to the pardon of the Father which returns us to eternal glory. This is the truth. But with painful appropriateness the return to glory and entrance into eternal exaltation will be accomplished only by way of the penance of falling again into dust, this time the dust of nonanimation that is assuredly a humiliation and degradation for the noble creature that is man.

This penancing truth reaches out to all who love this dead person, this *non-anima* that will so rapidly and appallingly forfeit its former physical testimony to *anima*. Those who are unwilling to mourn will strike out in fury against the truth of death. The unpenitential will hate death, fear death, execrate death. And all of these are, of course, precisely wrong responses to the penancing truth of death. Even farther removed from the right response are those who perpetrate frauds about death. We have the kind of cemetery that Evelyn Waugh observed and memorialized with such penetrating brilliance in his book, *The Loved One*. Fountains flowing, soft music playing, dummies reposing in a playtime park of unreality. We have a thousand devices to distract us from death, even to the inane scheming to withhold from the dying the fact of their dying.

Over and against all this bitterness and fear or this escapism through fantasies themselves crumbling and decaying with the odor of that worse death which is untruth, stands mourning pure and undefiled in its right response to penancing truth.

We have deserved to die and to experience temporary spatial separation from our loved ones as well as personal physical decomposition. And so we weep. It is an act of faith, really. A humble acknowledgment that we have brought upon ourselves a penance in altering God's original design. We accept and embrace the truth without acrimony, with tears but not with protesting screams, for there is nothing to protest about. This is always characteristic of the true mourner. He does not protest. He suffers.

Lazarus's sister, Mary, wept at home. And when Jesus came, she immediately got up and went out, not to accuse Him for allowing death to be, but to meet Him whose power she acknowledged. Martha did not berate the Lord, but merely stated a fact: "If thou hadst been here, my brother had not died" (John 11:21). That is, she made an act of faith in Christ's absolute authority over life and death. That she was mourning and not demanding a miracle is obvious in her concern over what seemed to her the imprudence of the Savior in preparing to present to the senses of the onlookers the humiliating facts of death. Better to leave poor reeking Lazarus sealed in his tomb until that last day when "I know that he shall rise again" (John 11:24). Meanwhile, with Christ, she and Mary did mourn the separation. And while Jesus did not accede to Martha's prudent counsel that He reconsider His plan, He did mourn: "And Jesus wept" (John 11:35).

So, too, did our blessed Lord mourn over Jerusalem, His tears accompanied by what is perhaps the most tender of all His self-revelations: "Jerusalem, Jerusalem, thou that killest the prophets, and stonest them that are sent unto thee, how often would I have gathered together thy children, as the hen doth gather her chickens under her wings, and thou wouldest not?" (Matt. 23:37). Here is another kind of mourning. That of the mother whose persevering love fails to reclaim the errant son. That of the shepherd who is so willing to leave the ninety-nine and search in the brambles for the one lost sheep, but whose bleeding efforts prove ineffectual before the determination of that sheep to remain lost.

That of the spender and giver and lover who is deserted by the heirs, unrequited by the donees, spurned by the beloved. Before the penancing truth of the self-destructiveness that is one option of the human will with whose freedom God has chosen to circumscribe His own omnipotence, Christ wept, "How often have I desired ..." God desired it. "And you would not." Man despised it.

With the parents through all ages who watch at the window like the prodigal father (Luke 15:20) but unlike him never see the wayward child returning home, Jesus shed tears. In company with all who see their best efforts go unrewarded and suffer unrequited love, Christ mourned. In God's own way, these mourners shall be comforted. And Christ Himself was "made strong" to go forth to His Passion and death even in the foreknowledge that of His beloved Jerusalem there would remain "not a stone upon a stone" (Luke 21:6).

Perhaps it is the will to go on that is God's comforting to this kind of mourning. "O, Corbie, Corbie!" mourned St. Colette over her native city that would have none of her. Then the Poor Clare saint went on with her work of the Franciscan Reform entrusted to her. "O Absalom my son, O my son," mourned David (2 Sam. 19:4). Then he got on with his business of reigning. "Jerusalem, Jerusalem!"

And blessed are all such stricken mourners. They shall be comforted.

We have said that the very antonym of mourning is self-pity. Those who mourn cannot at the same time indulge in self-pity. And those who are engrossed in self-pity will not be capable of mourning. Nor can they be comforted. For the self-pitying, it is not so much a matter of being weak, which we all are in one degree or another — "Who is weak, and I am not weak?" (2 Cor. 11:29) — but of pampering weakness, luxuriating in personal condolences. This has nothing at all to do with the mourning which Christ blessed.

Grief is strong. It will cry and weep before penancing truth. Self-pity will only whimper and whine. In the manner in which we face the penancing truth of our own misdeeds and betrayals of grace, there stands forth with bright clarity the difference between the simplicity of mourning and that whimpering self-justification that can construct almost incredible elaborations of non-truth. Let's consider the mourning for our own offenses.

We acknowledge the fact that we can defeat God's ambitions for our holiness, that we can belie His expectations of us. The mourning for our having actuated this knowledge is what we mean by that abiding contrition for sin that nearly all the classical writers on the spiritual life have presented as characteristic of holy creaturehood. The modifying specific is important: *abiding*. The very word has about it a kind of peace and even sweetness. The implication is steadiness, stabilization, and a form of contentment which, so far removed from anything masochistic, comes of recognition of the appropriate.

It requires healthiness of mind, robustness of spirit, and rectitude of conscience to be able to mourn for our sins. The moody melancholic is disqualified, for he does not really believe himself to be forgiven by God. The man flabby of spirit cannot manage anything like the true mourning for sin. He merely spins out his endless threnody from the easy chair of his caricature of spiritual living, disavowing God's ability to heal his wounds of sin in favor of the odious pleasure of perpetually examining his sores. The scrupulous are unequipped for mourning because they will never believe that God has really got the thing straight. If God knew about themselves what they know about themselves, God would undoubtedly withhold absolution. And so they march around and around in the stuffy room of self, intent on fetching up new evidence against themselves. What all of these non-mourners have in common is an undeviating focus on self. They simply never get as far as looking at God. This explains why they cannot see themselves either, except in the distortions that are their images wrested, as it were, out of the beam of God's love. And so it is that those who may appear to lament their sins and offenses, but are actually disqualified for mourning by their non-focusing on God, do some strange things. Maybe at this point it would be salutary, however, to move away from the more facile observation on the third person plural and humbly confront the first person. Let us agree that it is we, not any conveniently faceless "they," who do some very strange things and accomplish some very deft psychological sleight-of-hand work when we deliver ourselves over to self-recrimination, loud or listless as the case may be, according to mood, temperament, and weather.

We cannot have failed to notice that the person who makes the most noise about his condition of black-sheepedness is usually the most unwilling to be led to the sheep pool. Vehement declarations of our utter uncomeliness of soul often enough are used to avoid recruitment to holiness. We are no good, we explain and protest. Look at all our failures, laziness, betrayals — the lot. What we can really mean by this is that we do not by any manner or means intend to be deprived of our ticket to undemanding mediocrity. We are no good. So, don't expect us to be good. We are black sheep. That means that no one has a right to ask whiteness of us. We shall want to inquire of ourselves before God (for we get the oddest answers elsewhere) whether we have not written ourselves a license card for permanent or at least intermittent very bad behavior by signing in as a black sheep — as one determined to remain so. Certainly, there is no true mourning for sin in this.

So, too, in the indulgence of brooding remorsefulness, we can observe ourselves engaged in agile footwork to escape that confrontation with the penancing truth that elicits the right response of mourning for sin. If I convince myself, usually at full sound volume, that I am beyond recall and can never be worthy of forgiveness (as though anyone ever is), I give myself a kind of blank check on all manner of misdemeanors. The past is so bad that it is unforgivable. Obviously, this frame of mind will scarcely rouse me to great efforts in the present or splendid hopes for tomorrow. When we affront God's omnipotence and declare ourselves unforgivable, we grant ourselves permission to sin without limit.

There is something large about this, but in the sense of perversion. Or maybe we should call it inverse largeness that leads down to the sooty speck of a totally devital-ized self, devitalized since it is no longer recognized as the image of God. Because we affirm that we have done the unforgivably wrong in the past, we give ourselves permission to live without seeking forgiveness now. We excuse ourselves from mourning. We elect instead that bitterness of remorse that is often enough the springboard for all manner of licentiousness.

For the scrupulous, in their turn, there is obviously no possibility for mourning that is of its nature centered outside self and on the other. If we are centered on God, we of happy necessity believe not just *in* Him—but *Him*. We know that His power of forgiving remains forever greater than our power of offending. And we are given by Him to understand that He is not only in possession of all the facts of our life but apprised within Himself of all our vital (and non-vital, especially) statistics, and that He knows far more about us and our acts and our thoughts and our most secret desires than we do ourselves. We become aware of our sheer nakedness before Him. And in the midst of our tears of contrition and confusion and abiding sorrow for having betrayed God's love, in our mourning before the penancing truth, we are happy with an absolutely unique joy. We understand that we have never taken God by surprise. We are given to apprehend the shaking truth that God would not have repented His having created us had

He been able to foresee how we would function. For He did foresee. But one cannot go on describing all this. Anyone who has experienced it will understand, and it cannot be explained to one who has not. Mourning of this kind is less a mourning for our sins than for our sinfulness. And this abides with us always, not just concomitantly with desiring to have our sins forgiven, but made possible precisely because the sins are taken away and then only the consciousness of sinfulness remains, fitting us and inviting us to mourn that we may be comforted.

There are many causes for mourning. In the separation and loneliness that death occasions with the helpless witnessing of pain and suffering so far as concerns our power to change it, and in the abiding sorrow for our sinfulness, as in all other kinds of Christian mourning, there can never be an element of craven fear, though there is always something of the *timor Domini*, the awe before God who regulates life and death, who is judge in Heaven and on earth. The difference is very clear in the Latin words for these quite disparate and even antithetical fears. *Metus*, appropriately enough, is centered on me. I am afraid that something I consider adverse will happen to me, that something will be taken away if the truth is known about me, that I shall be brought up short, that I shall stand revealed. All that dreary company. God has nowhere promised that He will comfort this servile fear that has in it nothing of true mourning. *Timor, timor Domini*, is so different. It is, as the Scriptures explain, the beginning of wisdom (Sir. 1:16). It is of the Lord, yes. And it brings His comfort that will eventually release us into Love, for it is never centered on me, but on God. It is full of awe for God's power. It is informed with solicitude that He should not be offended. It is, especially, a right response to penancing truth.

Up through this beginning of wisdom that *timor* is with all its consciousness of creaturehood before Creator and offender before Love, comes for us that fullness of creature-hood and that understanding love that in the end, casts out all fear—even *timor*. God is love (1 John 4:8). *Metus* knows no mourning. *Timor* mourns and is comforted. And then there remains only *amor*.

We have lingered on Christ's mourning for His dead friend, Lazarus, and for His beloved city, Jerusalem. He shows us likewise in the Scriptures how He deals with the mourn-ing sinner. "Two men went up into the temple to pray..." (Luke 18:10). When the publican put down His stricken head and said, "O God, be merciful to me a sinner" (Luke 18:13), he did not add one word of justification. Mourners don't. How differently the story could have been written.

I am a victim of circumstances. If only I had had different parents. I got in with the wrong people. The business of being a publican and cutting corners on tax collecting has been handed down in our miserable family. Of course I had to associate with riffraff. I was led astray. Society has betrayed me. But no, the publican made the briefest act of contrition on scriptural record. "God, be merciful to me. I am a sinner." "He would not so much as lift up his eyes" (Luke 18:13) to God—*timor Domini*—much less defend his self-justifying rights against God's invasion of salvation. Do we not see our Lord's relishing of this parable when He concludes with a ring of pride: "This man went down into his house justified" (Luke 18:14). What does justified mean? Made holy. If we want to be quite literal, we can say that this sinner went home a saint because he was so humbly honest in confronting the truth and making a right response to its penancing. He mourned. Nor does one show forth one Beatitude apart from others. The forgiven publican was forgiven because he was poor in spirit, because he was meek and without excuse for himself, because he was without any self-pity.

It is strange how deftly we sometimes eschew that *timor Domini*, beginning of wisdom. We could ask ourselves why we are so unwise as to try to defend our interests against God. Is He our enemy, then? Someone before whom we must justify ourselves as the unfortunate Pharisee in that same parable did, listing all our good points? There is obviously no place for mourning in this kind of performance. To think that we have no reason to mourn for our failures is to step out of the radius of God's comforting.

Christian mourning reveals ourselves to ourselves, whether in some external sorrow, that is, not directly pertaining to our interior spiritual life, or whether in the inner court of our being. To those who are sorry and suffer without remorse, without argument, without need to defend their interests against God or against those who represent Him, God says, "They shall be comforted." He comforts as He sees fit. And His most exquisite comforting is experienced beyond explanation. Surely we have all of us had this experience sometime: the moment in which God really lets us see ourselves as we are and not as we so hotly debate that we are, and in which we know in our own being the exhilarating joy that comes of this. God does not love me because I have this or that quality or turn in this excellent performance (cf. the elder son of the prodigal father); but I am lovable because He loves me. I am forgiven because He is merciful. And I am comforted because I have mourned, and not raged or brooded or bedeviled myself and my company.

This seems to be what the saints meant when they talked of the joy they experienced in their faults and their failings. They were not glad that they had sinned, but the headiness of recognizing what they were and that God forgave them set them singing even as they wept. They mourned. And they were comforted.

One final word. In true mourning, there is no aggressiveness. People despair, people commit suicide, people blaspheme God because they refuse to mourn. They are aggressors of God, so He cannot comfort them. But the more we mourn in this scriptural sense of allowing ourselves to be comforted by God in our bearing of suffering, the more fit we are to forgive others and to comfort them in their own mourning. It is a beautiful circle. And it goes on and on, right into eternity, where mourning is no longer comforted because it is crowned.

Blessed are they that
hunger and thirst after justice:
for they shall be satisfied

It is surely not difficult to see that the ability to mourn is a
kind of prerequisite for hungering and thirsting for justice.
If we are incapable of allowing God to evoke from us right
responses to penancing truth, we shall scarcely be prepared
to understand justice for the kind of good it is and the chal-
lenges it proposes, much less to have an appetite for it. For
there are types of hunger that need to be cultivated. The
hunger for justice is definitely one of them. We also need
to work up an appetite for true justice. Nor can we inter-
change these terms. Hunger and appetite are not the same.
One can really be hungry without experiencing any zest

of appetite. And one can stimulate and indulge appetite where there is no real hunger. The latter fact is explicated clearly enough, all around us. It is not all that difficult, for instance, to stimulate a crowd to shriek for justice, smite for justice, maim and wound and kill for "justice," where there is no true hunger for real justice and precious little understanding of it.

To hunger and thirst after justice outside oneself is possible only to one who hungers and thirsts after justice within himself. There has to be that determined dedication to setting things right within. And this is a work of prayer and of suffering. In promising satiety to those who hunger and thirst after justice, Christ was sounding first of all a call to personal holiness, a summons placing far greater demands on a man than promoting social reforms, and, being likewise the one absolute requisite for engaging in socioeconomic reforms, an absolute somewhat overlooked in many quarters and by an imposing number of organizations. This is obviously not to say that we must present ourselves as finished models of holiness before we can concern ourselves with working for the triumph of justice in the world. *We must?* As though we could! As if such a phantasm of sheer egocentrism could be good! It is only to say what comes first, what is the *unum necessarium*.

It is just to be sure that we are clear on what Christ was talking about in the fourth Beatitude.

This fourth Beatitude is perhaps the most easily misinterpreted of the eight. We do remember one of the earlier recorded agitators for a just division of labor? Martha wanted justice done to herself. If she was not calling for equalization of wages, she did sue for parity of working hours. Mary was busy at establishing justice within herself. And we recall Christ's immortal comment (Luke 10:42). Yes, there is more to this fourth Beatitude than may emerge from a quick perusal of our Savior's words. One has to study in prayer and humble self-confrontation before the lifelong witness of Jesus what He really meant by "justice," lest we be too facile in our personal exegesis, isolating a word defined according to our private choice among synonyms offered. One has to study from within the context of Christ's life.

Nor shall we ever be prepared to accept the stark blessedness of the eighth Beatitude unless we have fathomed something of the fourth. The man who comes to understand that he is blessed in being persecuted for the sake of justice is the one who has known the arduousness of trying to establish justice within himself, of hungering and thirsting and aching to be holy before the all-holy God.

In the end, one sees that what men are most frequently and most cruelly persecuted for is their holiness.

Who is a just man? St. Joseph comes rather immediately to mind. For, while we know very little about him, we do know that he was just. Joseph was "a just man" (Matt. 1:19). The Scriptures declare it cryptically enough, as though this is really sufficient to supply a full description. What does it mean? Maybe we could first consider what it does not mean.

When St. Matthew proclaims Joseph a just man, the evangelist is scarcely taking Gospel time, as it were, to eulogize Mary's husband as one who did not cheat in his trade, engage in party politics, or smile the facile lie to attain an end. This is no scriptural lyricism about a carpenter in Nazareth who did not put his elbow on one side of the scale when weighing out material, who did not pad any figures when drawing up the bills.

Obviously, Joseph did not do these things, but that he did not do them was a predictable effect of that inner rectitude for which the Scriptures exalt him. To establish this kind of interior rectitude, one must suffer. There are simply no two ways about this. Christ learned the human internal rectitude of obedience in a school of suffering (Heb. 5:8). We can scarcely expect to learn it elsewhere.

What we can always do, of course, is to elect to be spiritual college dropouts, waving earnest protest banners for freedom and playing back the tired old record that obedience inhibits personal fulfillment. This is certainly much less demanding, even if totally unrewarding. But that is really another subject. Back to justice! It, too, is achieved only in a school of suffering.

Even the dictionary has spiritual counsel for us, defining the just man as one morally pure: perfect and upright before God, as one whose conduct conforms to the principles of right. So it is first of all my conduct that I am to be concerned with. To convince ourselves that we hunger and thirst for justice because our preoccupation is an earnest and maybe even feverish concern about right conduct in others is utter delusion. The kind of inverted accent by which I establish myself as a disciple of justice because I agitate for others to do what is just is, among other things, the perennial ticket to personal libertinism.

Our blessed Savior had some very forthright words to say about removing the beam from one's own eye before getting upset about the mote in another's eye (Luke 6:42). And even should it be rather clearly manifest that this is a case not of beam and a mote but of two imposing beams, it remains true that the first business on the agenda is removing one's own specific beam from one's own squinty eye. It can be surprising how differently we feel about that beam, real or supposed, in the other's eye after we have sweated and suffered and wept and groaned in our efforts to remove the persistent beam from our own. For one thing, we become gentle.

One can scarcely be harsh to a man who is not too magnificently successful in getting rid of his prejudices, psychological obstacles, inherited predispositions to wrong, and all the rest, when one is having a thoroughly exhausting time laboring to cast out one's own equivalents of the other man's beam. In fact, the other man's beam begins to appear more moteish.

The Pharisee in the familiar Gospel parable (Luke 18:11) sought to exalt himself at the expense of the publican with whom he smugly compared his estimable self. For this we experience the healthy reaction of hearty distaste. We do not feel that we would like to linger over tea with the Pharisee. It is all too easy to predict the trend of the conversation. But we want to remember also that the publican did not condemn the Pharisee. What a wearisome scriptural vignette that would make: the Pharisee thanking God he is not like the publican; the publican mouthing his own *Te Deum* that he is not like the Pharisee!

Blessed are they that hunger and thirst after justice

A hunger and thirst for that personal justice which is holiness unfailingly begets a gentleness toward others, a kind of horror of condemnation. The publican so hungered after justice within himself that he could only make the one appropriate cry of hunger: "O God, be merciful to me a sinner" (Luke 18:13). This is the beginning of holiness, the initiation of the reign of justice within oneself: the acknowledgment of sinfulness. "Have mercy on me" is the plea of the man thirsting for justice. And he shall be filled. Jesus made that clear. The publican went home "justified," filled, slaked. If he thought at all of the Pharisee and that poor fellow's odious listing of his own excellences, we are surely making an educated conjecture if we feel that his thoughts were gentle and compassionate. The unerring sign of the forgiven man is the need to forgive all other men. Not just desire but need. It is the sign of the coming of the kingdom of justice and truth described for us in the Preface for the Solemnity of Christ the King.

Then, for another thing, we grow in hope by our efforts to establish justice within ourselves. The hunger for personal holiness before a God all-holy is already His gift. We just do not get hungry in this area on our own. If there is blessedness promised to those who hunger and thirst after justice, we need to remember that the very hunger is already a blessing and the anguish of this thirst itself a precious favor from God. Christ did not say: "Blessed are they who have their fill," but "Blessed are they who hunger and thirst." And the more filled they are, the hungrier they shall be. This is His subtle ongoing blessing which is yet revealed to the most obtuse of us if we allow Him to enlighten our denseness with that revelation always gratuitously given and never earned, much less deserved.

The experience of our own yearning and aching to be what we are not yet, and this despite the findings of humble self-confrontation before the Truth: that we have a long and inglorious record of unholiness, interior injustice, fires us with hope for others as nothing else can quite do. We are robed in invincible hope for the breakdown of bigotry, prejudice, ill-gotten gaining and all the rest when we are humbly aware that it is possible to be highly unjust within oneself and yet hunger for justice, manifestly unholy while aching for holiness. We see this functioning in ourselves. One of the deductions we make from being hungry is that we are not full. Maybe we progress to a further deduction that our frightful emptiness of justice is necessitated by our repletion of indulged selfishness. We are malnourished in holiness because we are so full of self-husks.

The "hopeless bigot" no longer looks hopeless to the man struggling with the beam in his own eye, knowing the long duress of labor to remove it even with all the levers of grace operating, knowing even the difficulty of seeing the beam that is there. An eye with a beam in it can hardly qualify for twenty-twenty vision. It's a marvel it sees at all. A marvel of grace. A marvel that fills us with hope. The world can, after all, be saved. Evil can laboriously and gradually be overcome with good. Men can convert. The man blessed with that tormenting hunger for justice within himself knows this. He says: Look at me!

Returning to Joseph the just man, we observe in the Scriptures how he anguished to establish and maintain his inner rectitude. In the presence of a mystery he could not fathom, he did not angrily or otherwise demand an explanation. He did not protest, although he very understandably could have. He hungered to do what was right. And so he was filled. It was revealed to him what to do. And much more was revealed to him: a revelation given this precisely and directly, as a matter of fact, to no other man. The blessedness of his suffering hunger and thirst after justice in himself, for Mary, for God, gave way to the blessedness of being nourished and filled beyond what anyone could have predicted. His concern was that he himself should do what was right before God. That is what was clarified for him. Joseph was driven by desire for the establishment of justice within himself. That is what was filled.

If we really hunger and thirst after interior rectitude, inner justice, personal holiness, so that God can fill us, then we want everything that shows us the truth about ourselves. Here we return to an earlier point: we cannot be nourished and filled with truth if we are deliberately harboring untruthfulness within ourselves. The more receptive we are, the more uncluttered we are so that we can be receptive, the more we shall want anything that gives us to understand what is lacking of holiness in us. This is proof that we hunger and thirst. We hunger and thirst to be corrected as a person who is driven in an art, one who yearns to do better. The man who aspires to be a great sculptor hungers and thirsts for the master to show him his mistakes. He does not want to present the angular marble which he has never really malleted into a curve and hear the master say, "Well, that's good enough; that's all right." No, he hungers and thirsts to be told that he can do better than that and to be shown how. He is avid for correction. Christ has promised to satisfy such hunger and slake such thirst on the spiritual plane.

The fourth Beatitude cannot be assumed as a slogan for philanthropists, much less for agitators. It is an excellent thing to desire and labor for lifting oppressions from the poor, for championing the cause of the underdog, leading forth the prisoners, safeguarding minorities. But it is not precisely to this, good and wonderful as it is, that God is promising His banquet. The way He expresses the work of the promoter of justice is clear enough in Isaiah 42. Let's take a look at each verse of that passage:

> I have given my spirit upon him, he shall bring forth judgment to the Gentiles. He shall not cry, nor have respect to person, neither shall his voice be heard abroad. The bruised reed he shall not break, and smoking flax he shall not quench: he shall bring forth judgment unto truth. He shall not be sad, nor troublesome, till he set judgment in the earth: and the islands shall wait for his law. (Isa. 42:1–4)

It first of all emerges that the one who will bring true justice to the nations is the one endowed with God's Spirit. There are many spirits about, and there have always been many spirits about. Not all of them are identifiable with the Holy Spirit. The spirit of worldliness, my own wayward spirit, the spirit of anarchy, to say nothing of the crowds of evil spirits we have always with us — these are only a sampling of the myriad spirits calling for our attention and making pretense of their being the spirit of the Lord God.

The thing is, the voice of my own spirit can sound surprisingly like the voice of the Holy Spirit if I am not all that keen at discernment. The voice of my own spirit has so many appealing qualities; it tells me with the kind of modulation most acceptable to me all the reasons why it is excellent and praiseworthy to do whatever I want to do. So winsome a voice would just have to be the voice of God.

There is a great deal of insistence today on obedience, meaning that I obey the spirit. Right. Only — whose spirit? There was an old-fashioned term, now largely fallen into disuse, by which obedience to a certain spirit (my own) was called "self-will." The New Enlightenment disdains this uncouth appellation in favor of drifting in and out of supposed lifetime commitments, wandering from one "perpetual" promise to another, and juggling pledges like gilded balls in the name of obeying the spirit.

God's Spirit is given. It is never fabricated out of myself. Does not this passage in Isaiah foreshadow the fourth Beatitude to be revealed in the New Testament? What does it mean that God endows a man with His Spirit so that man can bring true justice to the nations, if not that God gives to that man the gift of hunger and thirst for justice? It is given, never contrived. That is why it is blessed. And one must have become practiced in listening through much prayer in order to hear the voice of the Spirit. God's voice never clamors for our attention. That may be one way of learning to distinguish the voice of our own spirit from the voice of the Spirit of God. We make much interior noise, and often enough it is externalized as well. God speaks in a low voice. An insistent voice, yes; but it is a low insistence. He does not shout us down. Nor does the man endowed with His Spirit shout others down. Isaiah goes on to remark: "He shall not cry, . . . neither shall his voice be heard abroad" (Isa. 42:2). This is rather a different picture of the man who is to bring justice to the nations than the image with soundtrack to which we have become accustomed.

God's man, hungering and thirsting for justice, does not break the bruised reed or quench the smoking flax. That he does not is less an expression of genial benevolence or natural pity than it is an effect of the personal suffering he has known in his own efforts to establish justice within himself. Anyone who has seriously and perseveringly worked to bring things within himself to right, who has known the demanding hunger for inner rectitude and the tormenting thirst to set things right within his own heart, has learned at what personal cost and with how many frustrations and depressions and failures the hunger and thirst for justice persist at all.

One can get very tired of hungering and thirsting for personal rectitude when there are other servings available. But out of allowing oneself to be blessed by God with this hunger and thirst comes a fountainous compassion for others. Is it not necessary to recognize oneself as a bruised reed, spent with effort and weak with many failures, in order to be concerned about other bruised reeds? Or, at least, that the concern be deep and effective? It is not enough to say: "Too bad!" One must soothe and nurture the reed that is bruised, raise it and strengthen it and coax it back to life and growth. Not enough, either, to cluck a pitying: "What a shame!" at the wavering little flame. It has got to be fanned and refueled. There has got to be work. And this comes out of humility and love, not out of shouting. Most of all, it comes from the prophet himself being faithful, as Isaiah observes. Faithfully hungry and thirsty for what is right, he brings true right. Otherwise, he brings something else. And we have heard that and smelled its acrid gun smoke and seen its patterns of blood.

It is needful to remember that those who deprive the poor are themselves the most deprived. They are the weakest reeds and the littlest flames. That justice be wrought in them and not just against them is the hope of the just man. Christ came to establish a kingdom of justice and love in the hearts of all men, and that included both the blind (and probably lousy) beggar, whom His apostles advised to take a detour, and rich Zacchaeus, who had many a change of tunic and never missed a meal and whom the apostles also thought out of order.

"He shall not be sad, nor troublesome, till he set judgment in the earth" (Isa. 42:4). That a man does not waver already implies that it is quite possible for him to do so. He has got to be crushable if his refusal to be crushed is to mean anything. The just man is himself vulnerable. That is why he is qualified to heal. He knows a wound when he sees it, wherever and on whomever it appears.

"And the islands shall wait for his law" (Isa. 42:4). Justice is a matter of law and not of lawlessness. It presupposes highly personal discipline and a hunger educated to know what alone will satisfy it, a thirst suffered that it may be slaked by living water. "The endurance of trial with unresisting tranquility is often a more searching test of courage," remarks Dom Aelred Graham, "than to meet opposition with direct assault."[5] It is also a sign of the just man, blessedly hungering and thirsting for universal justice.

Joseph was a just man. That is, he was holy. He had attained to inner rectitude by suffering. That is the only way for any of us. And unless we hunger and thirst for justice, right, holiness within ourselves, we had better not talk about establishing it outside.

[5] Dom Aelred Graham, O.S.B., *The Christ of Catholicism* (Garden City, N.Y.: Doubleday Image Books, 1947), p. 51.

Blessed are the merciful:
for they shall obtain mercy

All of the Beatitudes are humbling. And this is scarcely a thing to be marveled at. For the Beatitudes are Jesus' personally programmed Christian living. And He has told us the reason that He lived and loved as He did: that is, lived unto death and loved unto the end. "Having loved his own who were in the world, he loved them unto the end" (John 13:1). It was because He was meek and humble of heart. "Learn of me," He commanded us — if we can call so gently imperious an invitation a command — "because I am meek, and humble of heart" (Matt. 11:29). It is at least interesting and at most overwhelming that He really asked us to learn nothing else, implying among other things that it was going to elicit all our powers and exhaust all our resources to learn just that.

As each of us looks into his own proud and devious heart, it hopefully becomes obvious why there is no need to elaborate this truth. Let us just say that it is "significant" that Christ asked us to learn only one thing: to be meek and humble of heart. And invited us to learn it from Him because we are certainly not about to learn it from books, professors, or self-study; and no university is qualified to offer a degree in it. This is the foundation without which there is no true charity, no real grasp of truth, no enduring friendship, and not much of anything else, either. It would definitely, then, be a non sequitur if the Beatitudes did not underscore with their very blessedness this characteristic of the Heart of Christ.

Humility and meekness make for the flexibility of the poor in spirit who people the first Beatitude. In the second, we encounter meekness face on and spelled out for us. Again, one has to be humbled to be the Christian mourner of the third Beatitude. For you just do not make a right response to penancing truth when you are too blind with pride to recognize truth as having a frequently penitential outline and far too lethargic with pride's complacency to make that right response which demands energy. Neither does one hunger and thirst after justice, after the right-ness of holiness of the fourth Beatitude, without having breathed the good fresh air of humility. We have just talked about that. But now, as we consider the fifth Beatitude, we see the "surprising reward" perhaps more clearly or at least more immediately than in any other single Beatitude. "Blessed are the merciful: for they shall obtain mercy" (Matt. 5:7). The great good thing that is going to happen to those who show mercy to others is the discovery of how much they need it themselves.

The "mercy lines" of Portia to Shylock in Shakespeare's *Merchant of Venice* are famous enough and loved enough to invite still another quoting here. For the mental therapy administered by the recognition of a literary quotation almost never fails to be positive and even exhilarating. One does like to feel knowledgable! So, for therapy's sake, let us write the familiar passage out again: "The quality of mercy is not strained. It droppeth as the gentle rain from Heaven upon the place beneath. It is twice blessed: it blesseth him who gives and him who takes."[6]

Regaining our gravity after that therapy, we could reflect that most certainly William Shakespeare did not come up with this affirmation except after deep reflection on the

---

[6] William Shakespeare, *The Merchant of Venice*, Act IV, Scene 1.

fifth Beatitude. It is a quite expert bit of exegesis at the foot of the Mount of the Beatitudes. "It is not strained," Shakespeare avows. No, true mercy is never strained.

To be left unforgiven assuredly creates a more felicitous atmosphere in which to groan than to be "forgiven" at obtrusively high cost to the pardoner. This merely tends to raise the hackles of our pride yet higher. We shall likely produce in short order even heavier-textured material for mercy. Bluntly put, no normal person (a category in which we all hasten to assume our obviously rightful place) appreciates being forgiven "all over the place," so to speak. So, obtrusive "forgiveness"—no. But *obtrusive* is something divergent from *manifest*. For the high cost of Christ's pardoning and redeeming was a manifest mercy. Blood streaming out, eyes glazed over with pain, limbs convulsed—manifestations like these cannot be anything but manifest. But there was nothing obtrusive. To this author, one of the most heart-shattering passages in all Scripture is that enshrining Jesus' words to the depressed, distraught, and dense disciples on the road to Emmaus after the Crucifixion: "Ought not Christ to have suffered all these things, and so to enter into his glory?" (Luke 24:26). Ought not...? It is as though our blessed Lord waves aside the whole terrible tragedy, all the humiliation, all the shame and ignominy, all the desertion and betrayal, all the agony of body, mind, and soul—everything. "Ought not I to have done this?" The tone of the passage seems to imply: "these little things?"

And to enter into the glory of the Resurrection—not just His, but ours also—well, "ought not Christ...?" With all the reverence of one's spirit, one could dare to say that it is as though Christ said to those poor limited disciples almost as dull and uncomprehending as we are ourselves: "Oh, that?—that was nothing!" That is the way of mercy. It is not strained.

It is piercingly significant that Jesus did not say to the two en route to Emmaus: "Well, look what Christ went through for you! Look at the mercy He showed you! Look at the cost!" Could that ever have broken us to pieces like the love so great it waved away Passion and scourging and bitter crowning, spittle and sweat and gore with that "Ought not...?" We become one with Peter kneeling before Jesus after His manifestation of miraculous power and suggesting the imposition of the most terrible of penances as consonant with the personal history of Peter: "Depart from me, for I am a sinful man, O Lord" (Luke 5:8).

The fact that Peter by no means actually wanted Jesus to leave him in no way lessens the truthfulness and sincerity of his self-findings indicative of a parting of the ways for Christ and sinful Peter as being eminently appropriate. It was Peter's understanding that what Jesus could and should appropriately do was to turn His back and walk away that qualified Peter for the remission of the appropriate in favor of the gratuitous. Mercy is never "appropriate." If we feel for ourselves on the receiving end that it is, we are already disqualified to receive it because we do not understand it. So, too, it is only when we realize in our intellect and proclaim in our heart that truly Christ ought not to have suffered for us as He did, that we are prepared to go quite filled with gratitude and joy that He did. On our own frequent escapes to our multi-situated Emmaus, we have to be first at variance with Christ in this dialogue of "ought not?" before we can dare to agree with Him. One knows Him in the breaking of the heart as in the breaking of the bread. One can then venture into the land of mercy where all is given and never deserved.

Mercy unstrained, prodigal, modest — this is what fetches up out of our darks and deeps the realization of our need for mercy and how totally unmerited mercy always is, if it really is mercy. "It is not strained," Portia instructed Shylock about mercy. Taught by the Scriptures, we could add: "It is modest." Mercy is never ostentatious, although philanthropy can be. Mercy cannot be delivered with speeches or set to cymbaline accompaniment. "Let not thy left hand know what thy right hand doth," our blessed Lord said of almsgiving (Matt. 6:3). Mercy is the most basic alms of love. Its coins are forged in the heart, silently, almost secretly.

Once we start making considerations about mercy, calculating whether it is deserved, what measure should be given, we have already introduced into our thinking that strainedness that is totally uncharacteristic of true mercy. "It drops like the gentle rain from Heaven." We see how the rain drops and where. Upon flower and weed, soil and gravel, hill and valley. Prodigally, it falls into the river that may or may not seem to need it, as well as on the parched land cracking for want of it. He "raineth upon the just and the unjust" (Matt. 5:45). It should not require a lengthy consideration of that revelation of God's ways with man for us to conclude that it would scarcely follow that we should do careful sortings-out. Mercy to be mercy has of its nature to stream out all over. We shall never be merciful to one and unmerciful to another. For the reality of the latter act would, among other things, indicate that the former was merely an act of self-gratification or even of self-aggrandizement and vainglory.

"Like the gentle rain ..." The examples of God's mercy in the Scriptures are multiple. There is the adulteress of whose guilt there was no question (John 8:3–11). There is also no question of her contrition before the face of Christ, for sin can be remitted only from the acknowledged sinner, even though the acknowledgment of sin has variant forms and can also be merely a kind of formless groping, aching, wondering, intuiting. "Go and now sin no more" (John 8:11). Mercy never seeks to impose penalties or to lay on burdens. That is why the intrinsic "penalty" for receiving it is so great and the burden of responsibility assumed in accepting it is so enormous.

The insistence of mercy is in its very lack of insistence as we might understand it. Jesus did not demand of the woman: "How many times? Why? Where? When? Who?" and then impose a suitable penance. (What, just by the way, can be "suitable penance" for having offended God?) It is part of mercy that it evokes in the forgiven one a desire to do penance. A desire also to answer those un-asked questions, though not to linger on the answers as the determinedly self-centered insist on doing. Mercy elicits from within the other rather than adjudicates of itself. Yet, in this very gentleness and prodigality is the sheer sweep of the invitation. "Go, and sin no more." Do we realize what Christ asked of the woman? No more sin. Sin—no! No more. Not ever. None at all. In other words, Jesus said to someone whom we might not consider an outstanding candidate for sanctity: "Go, be a saint."

We shall want to look up this woman in Heaven, where we hope, through God's mercy to ourselves, to meet her and marvel at what was wrought in her by that same mercy. Then, there is the exuberantly sinning son of the prodigal father (Luke 15:11–32). We can never hear the story often enough; nor shall we ever fully comprehend the un-strained-ness of the paternal mercy as it waited at the window for the hour when it could release its gentle, saving floods. But there are two points in this incomparable vignette of mercy that we may not sufficiently reflect on or marvel at. One is the mercy to the elder son who tends to annoy us so. He is the toad in the lunch basket, so to speak, the swarm of gnats on the idyllic scene. It is at least "interesting" and at most highly informative about ourselves that even as we may be blinking back tears at this Gospel parable, we find ourselves readier to be aligned with the wanton younger son than with the elder paragon of perfection. I submit that we have something to learn about ourselves and about mercy from our easy contempt for the righteous older son and our ready simpatico for the younger. It is sometimes easier to show mercy toward the uproarious sinner whose roar has run down than toward the narrow-souled who have need to have their banks pushed back by flooding mercy. And so the father went out to the older son, too.

"Son, thou art always with me, and all I have is thine" (Luke 15:31). No annoyance. No scolding. No straining. The same mercy. The same love. We like to hope that the elder son did come into the feast after all, kiss his brother, and dance the whole night long. We shall want to look him up, too, God's mercy having arrived us one day at the Heaven where we shall find all the millions of elder sons saved and made large-souled by mercy.

The other point is, again, about that "intrinsic penalty" and that burden of responsibility that come out of mercy. Maybe I could be permitted to quote myself from a poem written about the Gospel prodigal and the each-of-us prodigal.

> The first robe, Christ, has crushed me with its
>   awful
> Weight of mercy. How these sandals pierce
> With little nails my feet grown great with roaming.
> And through what scalding sweetness of new tears,
> I see the ring securely on my finger
> Gleaming—gleaming too bright.
> I close my eyes.[7]

[7] Mother Mary Francis, P.C.C., *Where Caius Is* (St. Bonaventure, N.Y.: The Franciscan Institute, 1955), p. 35.

There is always the intrinsic penalty of that "awful weight of mercy." If the son had been granted his plea to be a servant, there could have been a solacing and perhaps a gradual diminishing of the sense of sinfulness, though remorse and bitter self-recrimination could likewise have been increased. This is not possible in the restoration of the "first robe" of innocence. True, we can soil it again or sell it again or tear it up again; but this will be a new choice. Innocence returned to us by mercy brings a new and terrible awareness of gratuitous love that closes off multiple options and leaves us only the primary alternatives of holiness or a return to the wallow.

"The bones that have been humbled shall rejoice," says the psalmist (Ps. 50). This is what mercy does. It crushes in the manner of an embrace, as the prodigal father crushed the sinful younger son to his heart and—who can doubt it?—the sulking older son as well. This is a new and different facet of the crushableness we spoke of when reflecting on the fourth Beatitude. But here, again, in a variant modality, one must be crushable in order to be crushed and rejoicing. "I see the ring ..." It is the bright insistence of my responsibility as the forgiven one. Not everyone is willing to bear this responsibility. And if I can "close my eyes" before the dizzying splendors of newly imposed responsibility as I gather up my God-restored inner strength to bear it, there is another way of closing my eyes, which is in order not to see. "If only you would not forgive/ Then I could stand tall" (ibid. — same poet!). Tall enough not to see, among other things, the other sinners and strayers and seekers around me.

And there is Zacchaeus, too (Luke 19:1–10). He may have had some half-smothered conscience rumblings to the effect that he should restore to those he had defrauded the sums that rightly belonged to them. Shown mercy, mercy raining all around and over him, mercy inviting him out to dinner, he restored fourfold the losses of his victims. Let us repeat it: the first mercy that the merciful receive is to realize how much they are themselves in need of mercy. However, the realization is not only of a present need, but also of a preexistent Sheolic inner state in which light neither probable nor even humanly possible has appeared.

We could put it this way, too: the blessedness of the merciful is not only to discover that they need mercy, but to be made aware that they have already received it. That we can be merciful at all is possible only because we have already received mercy. It is in fact the proof of it. We remember the Gospel account of that woman who "had a bad name in the town" and how Jesus commended Simon for his intelligent reply that the one who loved more was "he to whom he forgave most" (Luke 7:42–43) and then went on to remark of the woman that many sins must have been forgiven her "because she hath loved much" (Luke 7:47). The overflowing love of sincere contrition, like mercy, is possible because one has already been forgiven. "He hath first loved us" (1 John 4:10). Yes, that is why it is possible for us to love both Him and one another. He has also first been merciful, and that is why we have the blessed power to be merciful.

The blessedness has a kind of cyclic turning. There are vicious circles. This is a vital circle. God has been merciful. Therefore, we are blessed with the ability to show mercy. It has flowed into us from God, and that is the only reason it can flow out of us as a blessing upon others. Then, as it flows out, deepening blessedness is revealed: our own need of mercy. And the crowning blessedness is the assurance of always receiving what we give. "Blessed are the merciful: for they shall obtain mercy" (Matt. 5:7).

We could adjust Shakespeare's classic lines of description into a capsule of theology by simply omitting a word. "It drops as the gentle rain from heaven." That is what it is like. "It drops, a gentle rain from Heaven." That is what it is. That is what flows out of the blessedly merciful:

the mercy God has already given them. And so it can go joyously on, forever and ever. We have received. We give. We recognize our need to receive. We are qualified by this recognition to receive more.

"It is twice blessed: it blesseth him that gives and him that takes." It is not static. You have to take it just as you have to give it. It is quite possible to refuse mercy, just as it is unhappily quite possible to withhold it or, again, not to give it so much as to dole it out. And that takes us back to one of our first points. Mercy can never be doled out. You do not have ration tickets on mercy or for mercy. It is so free, so modest, so gentle. We may also need to recall to ourselves sometimes that we are just only when we are merciful. We say some odd things in our little stutterings about God, such as that He is merciful while we live, but He is just after we die. As though an unchangeable God, *immotus in se permanens* (hymn at None), had a kind of philosophical or theological wardrobe out of which He dressed for occasions! How could God possibly be "just" to us little fumbling, faltering folk, to us who can so deftly maintain a lifelong ambivalence of greatness and pettiness, high desire and low performance, easy pride and hard humility, to us in our multiplying ignobilities even as we elect nobility—how could God possibly be "just" to us except by being merciful?

Does not His justice demand that He be merciful to us, so puny, so feeble, so frail, so ridiculous? What is His mercy but the expression of His justice once He has decreed to redeem a fallen race that remains fallen even when redeemed? Of course, the truth of it is that He is neither just nor merciful but is rather justice and mercy. He does not exhibit attributes. We ascribe attributes to Him because we do not speak Divinity at all well. We are scarcely educated to express ourselves in the language of Pure Being, which has no terms. God is. And not merely as totality of all that is. Just—IS.

However, this is not to say that His IS-ness has not been communicated to us. We are created in His image and likeness (Gen. 1:27). "You shall be as gods," Satan promised our first parents (Gen. 3:5). The thing is, they already were. More, in fact. They were like God Himself—His very image, His own likeness. One of the very loveliest apparitions of God's IS-ness in us is our mercifulness. "God is in me, here abides," announce the merciful. The proclamation has no trumpet fanfare; it is as silent and as eloquent as a smile.

And so the IS-ness of God that we call mercy—and it is a good enough term since that is what Jesus the Word called it—flows out of us and flows into us more profusely than before because we have allowed ourselves to be enlarged.

Blessedness given freely to us, fountaining out, increasing within. A sense of our sinfulness ever increases, not to our despair or even to our despondency. "Jesus Christ came into the world to save sinners, of whom I am the chief," said St. Paul (1 Tim. 1:15). It was definitely not the expression of melancholia. It was the affirmation of a man happy to be redeemed and to be the stuff of concern for God's mercy. For it is so blessed a state to be in, this state of knowledgability that we need mercy and, having responded to others' need for it, we shall have our own need filled. And this by God.

Blessed are the clean of heart:
for they shall see God

Since there is scarcely anything more purgative to the drossedness of the heart than that humble receiving of mercy that makes possible the giving of mercy with the simultaneous new understanding of our need to receive it, it should not be surprising that our blessed Lord, immediately after proclaiming the blessedness of the merciful, should speak of the clean of heart. The humility indigenous to true mercy, whether given or received, turns out the pockets of the heart with all their accumulated hoardings and also scales pettiness off our being with a beautifully relentless blade. A new blessedness is revealed. "Blessed are the clean of heart: for they shall see God" (Matt. 5:8).

In a different sense than the immediate present fulfillment of the first Beatitude, "Blessed are the poor in spirit,
for theirs is the kingdom of Heaven" (Matt. 5:3), we find
in the sixth Beatitude, in a highly specific way, a future
reward brought into the present. Certainly, we shall all
have to be made clean of heart before we can see God.
We recall God warning Moses that he could not look upon
His face and live. "Thou canst not see my face: for man
shall not see me and live" (Exod. 33:20). And Moses was
likely considerably cleaner of heart than many of the other
children of Israel, then or now. Still, he could be allowed
only certain concessions, as it were. "When my glory shall
pass, I will set thee in a hole in the rock, and protect thee
with my right hand, till I pass: And I will take away my
hand, and thou shalt see my back parts: but my face thou
canst not see" (Exod. 33: 22–23). We also recall that after
Moses, thus "protected" from the face of God in order to
speak with Him, came down to the people, they were un-
able to support the sight even of such obliquely reflected
glory. And perhaps again some of those children of Israel
were better equipped to see the filtered radiance of God
than we are.

So, yes, there will have to be a totally cleansing process
for each of us to suffer before we can see God. Is Christ

then saying in this Beatitude, "Blessed are the blessed?"
Is He reminding us of what must be before we can endure
the unveiling of that eternal Beatitude that is the vision
of God? Hardly. It would not need a specific Beatitude to
announce that basic generic. So what did He mean? How
is that someday beholding of God's face announced in this
Beatitude? How is the future brought into the present? In
what manner shall the clean of heart discover God upon
earth? How does life practice for eternity? And then, who
are the clean of heart, anyway? What do we mean by that?
Whom did Christ mean?

We shall not want to take a restricted view of this Beatitude in which, surely, much more is meant than mere
physical integrity. To describe physical purity as "mere" is
by no means to imply that chaste stewardship of one's flesh
is not a most precious office, but only to remind ourselves
that something much larger and profounder is obviously
meant here by our Lord. The keeping pure of one's earthen
vessel is a part of the whole. It is a beautiful part of this
Beatitude, but it is not all of it. There is a virginity of the
mind, a cleanness of the spirit. Surely this is the Beatitude
of the unworldly.

We might call it the Beatitude of the transfixing gaze
that transfigures tragedies and joys, mountains and traffic

lanes, roses and stones, men and situations, all of a sometimes lithe and sometimes lumbering creation into its pure
and radiant nakedness wherein is discovered the firstborn
of creation, Christ the Lord (Col. 1:15). It is really only
the clean of heart who can love the world. For them there
is nothing to be puzzled over in Jesus' invitation to be in
the world but not of the world (John 17:16). No one is so
much at the center of the world as the clean of heart who
are not of it. For there are two aspects of the world. One is
worldliness, the other is reverence and compassion. Again,
one is total immersion, and one is stewardship. The clean
of heart know which is which.

If it is the total reverence possible only to virginity of
the spirit that transfigures all things into their true form, it
is the responsibility of stewardship, which returns substance
to otherwise passing phantoms, that alternately lures and
bedevils the unclean of heart and always ensnare them.
One cannot appreciate the world when one is moored
in it. You have to run free and eventually float free. The
unworldly are the only ones who have ever been able ef-
fectively to suffer with and for the world, to be in travail
with it until Christ is brought forth in the new creation
(Rom. 8:22). And certainly the unworldly are the only
ones who have ever been qualified to enjoy the world.

There is St. Francis of Assisi. So clean of heart, he sang
out the praises of creation without thinking it necessary
to consume creation, without needing either to execrate
or to worship it. His was the reverential love of the pure.
He saw God, and Him he worshipped. Everything that is
belongs to the clean of heart. And so he has no need to
be avaricious. Francis might be called frugal in his use of
creation to fulfill the needs of his own person, but actually
it was for him not so much a matter of fasting from feasting
as of feasting on his fasting. A little went a long way for
Francis because he possessed the whole way and the goal
besides. And this because he was so clean of heart.

Again, he did not wear a rough tunic because it was
all he had but because it was all he wanted. Nor did he
go barefoot in order to curse leather but because he knew
that he stood on the holy ground of creation and it was
fitting to take the shoes from off his feet. As a matter of
fact, no one is capable of forgoing leather unless he appreciates leather. Otherwise he would be only despising
it or, if sufficiently mean-souled, merely disliking it. One
has to have a very fine appreciation of food to be able to
feast on fasting.

Rather in the same manner that the meek possess the
land, the clean of heart roam royally free, continually

discovering God. Cleanness of heart gives us perspective on persons and things and situations so that we not
only see them in a new way, but we see what is in them:
God. Blessed are the clean of heart, for they shall see
God. Preserving this virginity of the heart (which takes
unrelenting effort), having achieved this purity of spirit
(and we want to remember here that recovering it after
having lost it is a new achieving of it), the unworldly
shall have revealed to them the meaning of the world.
They shall see God.

We are usually not comfortable while being cleansed,
but only afterward. Allowing God to cleanse one's heart
so that one sees not events but God in events, not just
persons to like or dislike or puzzle over or dismiss, but
God looking out of these persons—this requires a lifelong striving. Maybe we need to recall more often than we
sometimes do that the signs of the times are the signs of
eternity expressed in things present. If we simply observe
the signs of the times and stop there, we are missing the
point; in the deepest sense, we are even missing signs. For
a sign stands for something else. Signs of the times stand
for eternity in its present expressions. Anybody can see
the signs of the times. The clean of heart see through the
signs to the truth the signs proclaim, the direction they

give. They see God. The unworldly read divine directions in the signs of the times.

It can be helpful in laboring to become clean of heart to ponder what is characteristic of the clean of heart. Two primary characteristics stand out rather prominently. One of them is educability. Again we think of the meek, the teachable ones. The Beatitudes are not independent entities. It is a lovely word, that Latin *docibilis* out of which we create our "docile." And it is a real pity that so rich a word-concept should be in such general disfavor with the world. What is its frequent connotation? Someone who is weak. The supine person, the one with no ideas of his own. "She is docile," we say, often enough meaning that you could lead her along on a leash. All on the contrary, the truly docile person is the teachable person; and the indocile, the unteachable, one is actually the mule concerning whose mental prowess the psalmist set down an observation. "Do not become like the horse and the mule, who have no understanding" (Ps. 31:11). There can be for us on certain occasions at least a bit of amusement over the indocility of the mule, but it is really not at all a winsome quality in an adult biped of the human species.

Becoming very first-personal, I could fetch up an incident from my school days having to do with a student who knew very little but who was forever challenging the professor who knew a great deal. What Ms. Indocibilis produced in the rest of us in that class was embarrassment, a huge embarrassment. I really think she encouraged us to be teachable and clean enough of intellect to absorb some of the vast erudition of our instructor. Alexander Pope remarked quite some years ago that "a little learning is a dangerous thing." A blink of vision through eyes shuttered by unteachableness is another dangerous thing. We may think we are seeing when we are merely squinting. And it takes more than a squint to recognize truth, to see God. There was that summer day when Ms. Unteachable said once too often: "Can you prove it?" to the professor at whose feet the rest of us were extremely comfortable. And I shall recall here for the edification of any possible reader the exercise of stern self-discipline by which I managed that day to forgo asking my fellow coed in clear, resounding tones: "Would you be so kind as to shut up?"

The greatly learned are, of course, the happy con-verse — the docile, the *docibiles*, the ever more teachable. St. Thomas Aquinas described his tomes on which serious scholars through the centuries have fed as being only "a little straw." One has to know a great deal to know how little one knows. True scholarship makes for humility and cleanness of heart. Where these qualities seem to be rather notably absent, one has reason to be reserved about the depth of the supposed scholarship.

Two classes of persons found Christ at the beginning: the shepherds who knew very little of science but were clean enough of heart to recognize and be taught by an angel; and the wise men who specialized in scientific research and were clean enough of heart to be taught and led by a star. There is no record of the indocile finding Jesus. Those who know very little and think they know a great deal do not seem to be present. There was Herod, of course. Recordedly unclean of heart, he could not see God in a Child, but only a possible threat to his own unregal kingship. We could make a significant pause here to ponder a present rather widespread contempt of angels and a diminution of interest in fixing one's gaze on starry heights. In that brief pause, it may be recalled that cleanness of heart is not precisely the outstanding trait of our world society.

If we want it to be our personal trait, the first thing we shall want to do is to face ourselves in truth and discover in what areas of our lives we are not very educable. All of us have them. I doubt any of us would want to stand forth and affirm: "I am completely *docibilis*." The docility characteristic of the clean of heart is something for which we all need to strive. And to strive for it is in a measure already to have achieved it. By the mere act of confessing sincerely that in some areas I show myself not teachable, I am already conditioned to become teachable. I have achieved at least the beginnings of what I lack when I confess that I lack it. I open up.

The honest discovery and admission of a certain closedness, for example, is the beginning of openness. This is so far removed from the glib affirmation — insistence, really — on one's complete openness which invariably characterizes the impenetrably closed. Thus, in our times we observe the curious phenomenon of certain apostles of openness whose openness appears to be somewhat restricted. Openness only to oneself or one's attitudinal compatriots would actually seem to qualify one for a rather limited apostleship in this area.

The truly open and educable can be taught by anything. They learn from others, from situations. They can be taught perseverance by the bit of portulaca that comes perseveringly through the gravel. Maybe it doesn't get any water or any care, but it shows you what perseverance can achieve. This kind of educability was so evident in the saints. They were learning, learning all the time. Because they didn't have little stores of false erudition stacked up in their hearts, they were free to be clean of heart and open to God and men. One who knows little can question with acrimony, and another can answer with gentleness because he is so wise in his educability.

When we are clean of heart, we have flushed out, swept out all this clutter of false erudition so that it is possible for the heart to be clean. Even on the secular plane, no scholar would ever say: "I know all about this." The most eminent heart surgeon in the world will be the last to say: "I know everything about heart surgery. Just ask me anything. I have all the answers." We find in the context of daily life that the educable ones are those who are most clean of heart and that even, in the secular consideration, they always feel that they have so much to learn. It is self-evident that the more we learn about anything, the more we realize how much we still have to learn. A little learning is assuredly a dangerous thing. We cannot rest there. We never graduate intellectually, much less spiritually. This in no way implies that the docile and free of heart are not strong in their convictions, that they do not have ideals that never become obscured. It means only that they are open enough to learn God from others and from situations. The cluttered heart of the little-learning is not open to seeing God whose kingdom comes today.

The cleaner of heart we are, the fewer dark corners do we cherish in our heart for depositing ideas of which we are extremely fond and on which no other ideas shall be allowed to intrude. These are the dark corners to be illumined so that the light and sight of God can come in. If, when I am corrected, I have a stockpile of reasons to show my benefactor how wrong he is, if I am offered a new perspective and have another stockpile of false erudition for rejecting it, I am simply lost in my own clutter. I don't see God. I am dirty of heart in a deeper and much more dangerous way than in the sense of carnal impurity. What are "dirty thoughts?" Are they not less those engendered by the demands of nature or the insistence of men or the television of imagination than the satisfiedness that makes it impossible to see God? Let us repeat it: our blessed Lord certainly meant physical cleanness of the body and mental cleanness of thought when He proclaimed the blessedness of the clean of heart. But He meant more. The Scriptures expand His thought by many parables. We remember how the thieves and the prostitutes got into the heavenly banquet, according to our Lord's own forecast, and we recall who got thrown into the outer darkness and were left there to gnash their teeth. Look again at that prodigal son. The Scriptures say in very plain language that he had wasted his whole inheritance on harlots and loose living. Yet, in that exquisite scriptural vignette that is given us as a symbol of God's forgiveness, the boy was clean of heart. He was so humbled. He was so contrite. He became a penitent whose greatest hope was to be allowed to be a servant in his father's house. And that takes us over into the second shining characteristic of the clean of heart: truthfulness.

The prodigal son was physically unclean. He had been impure in the physical sense, and in just about every other sense as well, when he came to his father and said, "I am not fit to be your son; could I be a servant in your house?" At that moment, he was clean of heart. The bedraggled, hungry boy did not condition truthfulness. He did not say: "Well, at least I can be a servant here." He inquired if there was any possibility that he could be a servant. And what did the father who is the figure of God the Father do? He interrupted the self-accusations. You can see the finger of the father on the lips of the son. Really, he stopped the boy with a kiss and forgave him. And the son was made clean of heart. The proud and complacent are the really dirty of heart, and they do not see God.

There is another familiar scriptural passage that could be interestingly rewritten in the light of truth. It is the beginning of Genesis. Suppose at the initiation of that sorry tale, the serpent had not lied? The whole story began with untruthfulness. Then, Eve listened to the lie, disobeyed, panicked, and proceeded to do what human nature invariably seeks to do: she drew someone else into her predicament. Adam was easily enough drawn. But if the two had been clean of heart in contrition, how would the story run? When Eve said to God, "The serpent deceived me" (Gen. 3:13), one catches little undertones and overtones of her really blaming God for her whole downfall. Who created the serpent anyhow? Who put him into the garden? "The serpent deceived me." Suppose, instead, she had said: "Oh, God, forgive me! I was ambitious, I was vainglorious, I was so proud. I wanted to be You. I wanted to take over Your role." Suppose she had confessed: "I was so foolish. You gave me everything, and I listened to a snake. Have pity on me." Would Eve then have needed to be cursed?

Then, what of the happy supposition that Adam had said: "Oh, God, forgive me! I was Your first creation in Your own image. I should have been strong to help my mate. Instead of that, in her moment of weakness, I failed her. I am really all at fault. I am the one on whom she should have depended for strength; but I failed her, God, and I failed You." Perhaps the thorns and thistles of Adam's future lot and his bequest to all his progeny would never have appeared. The fallen can always regain cleanness of heart. They need only be truthful and contrite. For all of us, the implication of cleanness of heart is that we have been cleansed. Who shall stand before God and say: "Behold, your unspotted one!"

If educability and truthfulness are two outstanding characteristics of the clean of heart, there are also two special effects of cleanness of heart. The first is a great lightness of spirit. Like the peacemakers whom we shall next consider, the clean in heart are happy children of God. We see this joy very apparent in Francis and Clare of Assisi. They were so light of heart, "always joyful," as the nuns testified of Clare at the process of canonization. Joyful to be forgiven, light of heart to have met the truth and acknowledged it.

When we are always ready to be taught, are really truthful confronting ourselves before God, we have a rewarding sense of wonder. We can say to ourselves in Old Testament terms, just as Job did, "Yes, you maggot, you! You worm, you!" and still know that we are the beloved of God. It is not too attractive a prospect to witness to maggothood or wormdom per se, but to be a maggot or worm beloved of God is not uninviting. It is to be a very noble kind of worm. Who could mind being a worm cherished by the Lord? The cleanness of heart that comes of being teachable and truthful brings a reward not of depression or defeatism nor, much less, of despair, but of joy. In our acknowledged wormliness alone does our butterfly possibility lie.

A second effect of cleanness of heart is freedom. Here again we see clearly the interlockedness of the Beatitudes in the wholeness of Christ's love. For we have already seen the freedom which is the property of the poor and the meek. When we are not infatuated with our own opinions and judgments, we are prepared to yield them over when truth shows them up as charlatans. To be sure, the yielding up involves pain. Life is full of pain; learning is full of pain. Any learning. There can be a certain drive toward it, a kind of exhilaration; but there is also much labor and perspiration involved, much fatigue for mind and body. If pain is part even of secular learning, we can scarcely be surprised that it is often painful to learn the only thing God told us to learn: to be meek and humble of heart. It should not come as a surprise that there is a lot of work involved in becoming and remaining clean of heart. It is not a crash course.

We have our own opinions, judgments, evaluations. We are ourselves. But we are clean and free when our roots are not in any of these but in God. This seems to be what is meant in the Beatitude, "Blessed are the clean of heart, for they shall see God." See Him in eternity, yes. But they shall see through to Him right now, too. Of course, let us say it again, this takes more than just a bit of doing. We need to prostrate ourselves before God and ask Him: "Show me where I am unclean of heart. What do You want me to surrender that I may have the great reward of the clean of heart?" And we have to be prepared to let Him answer, and to realize that the freeing and happy rewards of truth come only to the truthful. The prodigal son doubtless had to work on himself so as not to say, accusing his father instead of himself, "Why did you let me go out, young as I was, into a wicked world? It is really all your fault." Poor Eve did the equivalent of that in a somewhat more subtle mode, but to God. "Why did You put the snake there? Things were going along so well before he came slithering along." The boy, truthful, humbled, educable, was immediately cleansed. Eve, less candid and only humiliated, needed long penancing to become clean of heart. No doubt most of us line up alternately with the contrite wanton son and the self-excusing Eve. For them, to be given the first robe of restored innocence or to be made mother of the human race, it was necessary to be cleansed and to see God. The unworldliness of the clean of heart is not lightly achieved. That bears repeating. The educability and truthfulness that make freedom and lightness of heart possible are never effortless. But the reward is great. We see God.

Blessed are the peacemakers:
for they shall be called the children of God

To be a peacemaker implies that we have already in some fashion seen God. Turmoil is ours. Peace is God's. It appears both in the Old and the New Testament as God's favorite light to diffuse and gift to bestow. *Shalom!* Peace be to you! It is also a very favorite cry of our times. Unfortunately, one might say that it is a favorite war cry. How many veins have stood out on how many heads in the name of "peace"! Sometimes it seems to be spelled out in vitriol. And then, again, it can be and often enough is the shibboleth of the lethargic: "Peace! Peace!" Each to his own. Let every man go his own way, by which seems to be particularly meant that he should keep out of mine.

It is neither the peace-stomper nor the peaceful sleeper of whom Christ proclaims the seventh Beatitude. He is speaking not of the destructive but of the creative, not of the nihilists but of the builders. This seventh one may qualify as the most active of the Beatitudes, that of the makers. Workers. Doers. Thinkers. "Blessed are the peacemakers: for they shall be called the children of God" (Matt. 5:9).

Maybe we would prefer that Jesus had said: "Blessed are the peaceful." And perhaps that preference is what has led us to pretend that that actually is what He meant. Only it isn't. Christ always said exactly what He meant. And He is identifying as recognizable children of His Father those who make peace and not those who propose to us peace as a sleeping bag for themselves.

Peace is not always easy to make. We have, in any case, got to have the ingredients. And they are found only in God. We never find peace in things or in circumstances or in situations; least of all do we find peace in ourselves. Yet how often we make the mistake of looking for peace precisely where it will never be found, where even our individual wry experiences have manifested that it is never found. In ourselves we have the deposit of Original Sin on which we have gathered the considerable dark interest of specific failures and personal blindness, but we do not have peace.

Just as every response to grace has left us a little clearer visioned, so every refusal of grace has left us a little weaker, a shade less focused on God, a bit more wanting in the ingredients for peacemaking. It is folly to go on rummaging about our faltering little selves for the strength of peace which is not *ex natura* resident there. It is not by settling down into the cocoon of myself that I shall find that personal peace that allows peacemaking to become a proximate possibility, but in emerging from that most wizening form of inbreeding that is self-complacency out into the light and vastness of God. It always comes back to that kenosis that Jesus taught us by His own manner of living. He "emptied himself" (Phil. 2:7). There are a number of accumulations of which we need to empty ourselves if we want to allow for the action of God-filling. One is our own folio of blueprints for our peace. Another is our battle strategy to win peace.

It is helpful to be good-humored with ourselves if we are to arrive at an honest assessment of ourselves. Better to be amused at ourselves than angry with everyone else because the edifices of peace that we have striven to erect from dubious blueprints always topple and yet never seem wholly to disenchant us from the desire to build again on exactly those same shaky foundations.

Surely there is no one who would not admit, "I have sought for peace on this or that occasion, perhaps on many occasions, in myself, in what I wanted, in what I was sure was the will of God. And I did not find it." Yet we have to confess that we continue this peace-hunt, always at our own expense as well as others'. It is not in getting our own will accomplished (to say nothing for the moment of our own willfulness) that peace is achieved. Presuming that we are all healthy of mind, we hopefully have experienced the spiritual enervation and even psychological decline that follow upon the spirited battle to "get our rights, get our wish, get our will" at the expense of others' rights, better wishes, nobler will. What we get is a sort of spiritual multiple sclerosis. It is a sorry spoil we carry off from some of our most pitched battles. Yet we can so quickly start girding our loins for the next war of aggression or colonization. The fact that we fail and fail does not seem particularly to deter us from the same doomed efforts.

It is humble good humor that will eventually arrive us at the point of making some lasting deductions, the most vital of which is that we shall never find peace in ourselves or in the ideal situations that we have decided are requisite for peace or in the circumstances that we maintain are peace-productive. It is the God-situation, if we may call it that, where alone peace is. Or, more simply, God's will. It is surrender to His blessed will, which alone is peace-productive. And a Franciscan poet pointed that out several centuries ago. "In his will is our peace," observed Dante Alighieri.

It is pleasant to mouth the words, but difficult indeed to induce the mind to give practical assent. Why is it so difficult? Rather, why should it not be difficult? God said, "My thoughts are not your thoughts: nor your ways my ways" (Isa. 55:8). It requires many an ill-fated forage into selfishness and many a wasted study hour with those personal blueprints for peace before we discover that Dante was right. And, more importantly, that Christ was right. "It is hard for thee to kick against the goad," Jesus sympathized with Paul's doughty efforts to do Paul's will (Acts 26:14). That could be paraphrased into the immediate source of Dante's conclusion. "Doing my will is your peace." And so we see St. Paul being led by the hand, a feat that very probably no one had accomplished since Paul passed his third birthday. And we notice something else: that when Paul stopped kicking against the goad, he began to suffer in peace.

Blind, stunned, covered with the dust of the Damascus road onto which he had so ingloriously and yet gloriously fallen, Paul of Tarsus began that lifelong process of kenosis that both gave him peace and allowed the ingredients for peacemaking to enter into him, and gave us the Apostle of the Gentiles. He had been centered on serving God by doing his own will. It is comforting somehow to reflect that great Paul suffered the same delusion we do: that, obviously, our favorite ideas must be God's will. Our own voice can sound so much like what we consider to be the timbre of God's voice. Then, too, our own voice has a normal volume of "high," which sometimes likes to overpower the low-pitched voice of God. Only the message gets through; and since it is all I can bear, I conclude that it has to be the sound of God. The sound of me can suggest strange conclusions simply by way of crescendo alone. These crescendos lead us away from peacemaking and have nothing at all to do with establishing filial relations to God. They do not make us His children.

That takes us right back to the educability of the clean of heart. One has to be educable if one is to become a peacemaker and be a blessed child of God. Not finding in ourselves any materials for peacemaking, we are happily almost obliged to look into God. That is already to have material for making peace. For the first ingredient of peacemaking is a total God-centeredness and God-givenness.

I become someone who relates to God, at once going out of myself and re-entering into the center of myself where He is, where He comes to my self-emptying. I leave off ambitioning to be the sun around which God is to revolve along with the lesser satellites of my planetary system who are my fellow creatures. We are talking now of becoming, of leaving off. It is comforting to know that the saints had also to leave off certain pursuits and abjure certain plans in order to become what God's will ambitioned them to be. Let us look at St. Francis of Assisi.

Francis's name is almost synonymous with peace, although his earliest ambitions were to make war on the grand scale. That is, he was to be the greatest knight, winning the loveliest lady, making the most historic forays, leading the noblest cavalries. These were all his own ideas. After God had revealed to Francis some ideas of God's own, the accent shifted to God. And so we find Francis at the very beginning of the orders which came to bear his name as Franciscan, not only making peace the hallmark of those orders but making the source of the hallmark very clear: "The Lord has revealed it to me." "The Lord gave me this greeting, that when the brethren meet a man, they are to say: 'May the Lord give you His peace.'" Francis had come to understand that peace was not to be achieved by war and, even more basically, that peace was not his, but God's. "His peace." The Lord's own peace. The only real kind there is.

When the followers of St. Francis increased, he would gather them about him for instructions. (One loves to picture the scene.) It went something like this: "Now here is what you should say when you go out to the people; and listen carefully, because the Lord himself revealed this to me, and it is His idea, not mine — say, 'May the Lord give you His peace.'" History describes for us how out of this instruction came the motto of the Franciscan Order: *Pax et bonum!* This was Francis's great burning message, his mission, to bring peace and all good to the people, peace and all blessings. And these from God. What this required first of all, of course, is that Francis would first have found them in God. He made peace very notably throughout his short earthly life, and the happy repercussions of his life remain clearly audible after centuries. Had Francis not been educable, never learned to discern the voice of God from his own voice, we should not have this irresistible little peacemaker to inspire everyone from Supreme Pontiffs to Leninists. One remembers the famous remark of Lenin that what the world really needed and only needed was ten Francises of Assisi.

When God set about teaching St. Francis how to make peace within himself so that he would be able to make it for others, He showed Francis the tawdriness of the baubles he was chasing after and the smallness of his ambitions. For us, though, it gives pause to note that even Francis's mistakes were on the noble scale as we would grade them. It was not that he wanted to be the richest man in the world, but the most gallant knight in all the world. And if he aspired to win the most beautiful lady in the world, it was going to be just one lady. But Christ showed His poor little one (as Francis would come to be known the world over — *il Poverello*) that even this was nothing beside what He Himself willed for him. "Francis, go and rebuild my Church." Francis got this message all wrong; and yet, he actually got it all right, because he was now looking for the peace of God's will and it did not matter all that much that he didn't quite assimilate God's idea. The important thing was that he now wanted only to actuate God's ideas.

So, while God was speaking to Francis about rebuilding the swaying spiritual edifice of the thirteenth-century Church undermined with war and luxury and carnality, Francis understood the message to concern dilapidated church buildings. What was important was that Francis was trying to understand, and that he set out immediately to do what some of us might quickly have explained to God was impossible. There could have been an instantly assembled brief for the defense: "I am a shopkeeper's son. I know a lot about cloth, but nothing about masonry. I never was strong, and You may recall that I've just been very ill. I am not built for hauling stones, a task quite beyond my muscular abilities. Furthermore, there are wars going on, and fighting is called for. It's no time, if You don't mind my saying so, for spending time pushing stones into the walls of disreputable little churches like this one in which I have been praying for a different kind of message than I'm hearing, God. And what about a committee? Shouldn't we consider tearing down this church? Have you studied the situation with your advisers?" Et cetera. Unlike what we might have said, Francis said nothing. Unlike what we might have done, Francis went right out to get some stones. He had been told that God willed him to rebuild His church.

He must have had a very difficult time with the stones which, incidentally, he had to beg, being at that time rather short on funds. Or, to be exact, penniless. But he set himself up in his own kind of business, which was to "pay" a blessing for one stone given and two blessings for two stones. In this kind of management, Francis was his own astute businessman, unique among men. There were other matters concerned with this "rebuilding of the church" that could be verified as worthwhile only by that peace that comes of surrendering oneself utterly to God.

Again, it is that first ingredient for peacemaking of which we have already spoken, the total God-givenness.

Francis was very happy hauling his begged stones, not because his back hurt or because people were making fun of him, but because he was making the glorious discovery of peace in God's will. We remember his own brother mocking him: "How much for your sweat, Francesco?" and Francis's at once good-humored, noble reply: "It is already sold to the Lord!" The new stonemason was happy because, as he thought, God had told him to carry stones. He had found peace in God's will, and it did not matter to Francis if this should prove to be what God wanted him to engage in for the rest of his life. What could we want to do with our lives, any of us, except what God wants us to do with them? They are His gift. One would hope to honor the wish of the donor. Then, there was the peace that permeated St. Francis's vibrant being because of his total givenness to the Church of God. When the amplitude of Christ's dictum about rebuilding His Church began to open before Francis and when he had attracted a dozen or so men to join him in his newly founded group of mendicants whom he would never have dared to call an "order," it occurred to the pope if not to Francis that they would do well to have a Rule of life. One can readily subscribe to the educated conjecture of Father David Temple, O.F.M., who suggested how this was probably done:

> Supreme Pontiff to Francis: "You have got to have a Rule."
>
> Francis to his brethren: "The Church says we have got to have a Rule. Somebody bring me a piece of paper, please. I have to write something down."

And from the whole evidence of St. Francis's life and death, we can just as readily conjecture what he would have done had the Church said: "No, you can't do it that way"; or "We will put your Order on trial for fifty years and perhaps then approve the Rule." He would certainly have replied, "All right." He would have set about living the fifty years (which actually his short life would not have proved able to accommodate) on trial.

None of this is to suggest that St. Francis was passive, permissive, or servile. He could say to his brothers with splendid simplicity: "The Lord has revealed it to me," just as he had remarked quite casually when imprisoned as a young knight: "One day the whole world will run after me," and as he was later to rebuke his spiritual sons less dedicated to their own first ideal than to innovation: "Do not talk to me of other ways, this is the way God has revealed to me," and just as, toward the end, he was to proclaim with the classicism of a Greek drama: "My order will endure to the end of time. God has told me." Francis was bold enough and simple enough to declare that God had spoken directly to him; and yet he submitted always, and with grace, to the representatives of God.

Francis had his own problems with the "institutional Church," but he had very different ways of solving them than some others. There he was with his God-given mission; yet he forbade his brothers to speak in any diocese without the bishop's permission. There is scarcely a man in all history more manifestly Spirit-led, but we do not find Francis overriding the hierarchy with loud cries of being led by the Spirit. He definitely did not say: "Listen here, I have this message straight from God. Down with dissenting bishops, down with institutions, down with the establishment." St. Francis was so established in God and in the peace of God that he was able to cope with the glaring defects of the ecclesial establishment of his times and go on busying himself, not with demolishing that establishment but with making peace in it, which is a decidedly more difficult thing to do. What price dynamite? Or the flagellation of the press? And, returning to the hierarchy, Francis had with bishops, as with the acquisition of stones, his own way of going about things. When front doors were closed on his intense little face, he hurried around to the back. And, in the end, he got in. He somehow always ended up in that bishop's cathedral, up in the pulpit.

"What will You have me to do?" This was the whole expression of St. Francis's life as of St. Paul's apostolic life before him. That is the question indicative of the total givenness to God and the absolute centeredness on God which allows for peacemaking. It would be helpful to watch Francis actively engaged in the peacemaking that personal surrender to God equipped him for effecting.

When there was a bit of trouble with the Muslims, Francis thought he had better look into the matter. Typically, he called upon the sultan. And this not to tell that worthy that he was a no-good sultan and not fit for pious Christians to walk on, but to enthrall the monarch with his simple efforts at peacemaking. Again, when the Bishop of Assisi and the *podestà* of Assisi were offering the townsfolk something less than an example of elevated fraternal charity, St. Francis realized that something had to be done without delay. He had a script all written for the occasion, and it did not run as some of ours might. There was no: "You cut a fine picture of a bishop, you do! What a spiritual leader you are!" No "Where's the collegiality? You are a menace to the Gospel." Neither was there any: "How did you ever get elected *podestà*? It must have been rotten politics!"

Francis just did not brood over the bishop's possible disqualifications for showing forth the meekness and humility of Christ or over the *podestà's* failure to delineate the features of the ideal mayor. He simply set out to make peace where it was wanting. He sent Brother Pacificus to sing them his new verses about peace. And we do love to picture those two fulminating Italian leaders melting into tears before this kind of approach and embracing each other. For that, as a matter of fact, is what they did. Francis had sent Brother Pacificus because he himself was then ill and suffering. And that brings us to the second ingredient for peacemaking. One has to be willing to suffer.

If we are to make peace, we have to know how to put ourselves in the background. In the little incidents of daily living that occur wherever human beings are gathered together, one has to become adept at silencing the voice of personal outrage if one is to make peace. Frankness and openness are excellent attitudes and expressions, unless by frankness we mean something in the nature of a tank rolling over human turf or the openness of a cannon mouth. When we are involved in one of those inevitable misunderstandings of life, there is a choice between inflating one's lungs for the predictable: "I said it as plainly as could be. Why don't you listen? You are always misunderstanding me and misquoting me!" or opting for the response of the peacemaker: "I guess I didn't make myself clear." It is such a small example, but an example of large concerns. And who is not disarmed by such a reply? One has to learn to suffer in small, secret ways before one is equipped for peacemaking.

Again, there is the matter of another kind of personal outrage: my splendid intentions are going unrecognized. How can somebody say thus and so when I have such a shining intention? How can anyone be hurt and sensitive when I mean so well? The more we engage in the peacemaking possible to the secret sufferer, the more we come to appreciate that what is important is that I hurt someone, that I need to see what in my manner of expression does not deliver the goods of all these splendorous intentions of mine, that I need to explore my own manners.

One doesn't become a peacemaker by meditating on what a great, dedicated person one is, and how unappreciated and misunderstood by the lesser brethren, but by taking on oneself the meekness of Christ. "If I have spoken evil, please tell me what it is. If not, what is the problem?" (cf. John 18:23). That somewhat paraphrastic expression of the words of Jesus, who had just been slapped in the face by a servile churl, could well be written into our *Handbook for Peacemaking*. There is no humility without suffering. Only pride comes painlessly. And there is no peacemaking without suffering. We all want to spread peace, unfurl it like a banner; but "maker" is the key word, and a very demanding one. Yet, there is another perspective on the suffering and the pain; it is good to remember that pride is painless—until afterwards; and the humility needed for peacemaking is painful—until afterward. The lasting rewards exchange places with the conditioning elements.

It is a wondrous thing to bear a family likeness to God. And that seems to be just what our dear Lord is talking about in the seventh Beatitude. He himself found His peace in the Garden of Gethsemane in doing the will of His Father. There alone we shall find ours. And out of the God-givenness that expresses itself in utter dedication to the divine will and out of the willingness to put ourselves aside is created the capacity to receive the ingredients for making peace. It can seem more inviting to "feel" peaceful than to make peace. It is easier to recline than to work. But Jesus blessed the workers and makers and gave them the right to bear the name of their family resemblance. They shall be called the children of God.

Blessed are they that suffer persecution for justice' sake: for theirs is the kingdom of Heaven

We arrive at the final Beatitude to find ourselves again confronted with immediacy. As in the first of His proclamations of those who are blessed in God's sight and among men, so also in the last, Christ makes His declaration an already present glad urgency. "Blessed are the poor in spirit: for theirs is the kingdom of Heaven" (Matt. 5:3). And now: "Blessed are they who suffer persecution for justice' sake: for theirs is the kingdom of Heaven" (Matt. 5:10). It requires no great mind-wrenching to understand that our blessed Savior is establishing a special relationship between the poor in spirit and those suffering for their God-given convictions.

One really has to be poor in spirit to be equipped for salvific suffering. Jesus Himself had to renounce the holdings of His own human will and to disengage His decision-making from the revolt of His human intellect in the Garden of Gethsemane before He was humanly poor enough to suffer for the divine redemption of all men. There is a very definite follow-through from the first Beatitude to the last in which those suffering persecution are joined with the poor as having the kingdom of Heaven even now, in time. "The kingdom of God is within you" (Luke 17:21). When you are poor. When you are suffering persecution for the principles of life and holiness. In saying that there is a follow-through from the first to the eighth Beatitudes, we are already defining the eighth.

The etymology of the word "persecution" seems rather startling at first consideration. And this is probably because the exposed core of truth is bound to be stunning in a soporific company of half-truths and popular delusions. *Per* and *sequere* (*secutus*) are the Latin words from which devolve our "persecution." Quite literally, "to follow through." To attain to that fullness of moral purity that justice is, one has to suffer the follow-through of everything Christ has set forth in the other Beatitudes, beginning at the first.

We reflected in chapter one that to be poor in spirit and possess the kingdom of Heaven, one must agree to be vulnerable. We recognized that the poor in spirit must deliver over to others the power to hurt them, since without this there is no loving. Could we say it again? One has to let oneself be exploited and misunderstood, for this belongs to loving. The completely poor in spirit are the utterly hurtable. Christ had no defenses against ingratitude, misunderstanding, denial, desertion, treachery. He was poor enough to love on.

We have also considered at what painful effort the strength specific to the meek of the second Beatitude is gained, and with what taxing practice their reposefulness is achieved. And in reflecting on the mourners whose blessedness is proclaimed in the third Beatitude, we saw that mourning is a right response to penancing truth, a response made possible only by suffering freely. But it was in our meditative study of the fourth Beatitude, when we investigated justice as actually being what even the dictionary purports it to be: moral purity and uprightness before God; and the just man as being the one whose conduct conforms to the principles of right, that it became very clear that we shall not be prepared for the stark blessedness of the eighth Beatitude unless we have fathomed something of the fourth.

That inner rectitude that is the first and basic justice for which Jesus declares it a blessed thing to hunger, is not achieved without perduring suffering. Manifestly unholy while sincerely aching for holiness, we discover that we are hungry for justice. We can prove it. A deduction we make from being hungry is that we are not full. The body testifies to its hunger for good by producing in us a stomachache.

Then, for those merciful ones who are declared blessed by the Lord and promised mercy for themselves, there is again the vocation to suffer. Each Beatitude is proclaiming, along with the blessedness specific to its own focus of concern, the absolute necessity of suffering in order to achieve any of the goals God ambitions for us: poverty of spirit, meekness, right responding, yearning for justice, mercifulness. There is a "persecution," a follow-through of suffering in all of them, as they unfold their mysteries of the spirit and simultaneously invite us to the ultimate discovery of the final Beatitude. One is not truly merciful at no cost to himself. Nor does anyone dispense real mercy after the manner of an enthroned monarch distributing alms to the poor. Mercy is given to the poor only by the likewise poor. Interacting, overlapping, repeating, revealing: this is the way the eight Beatitudes proceed. There is the follow-through of each to the other and on to the culmination of the eighth in its triumphant climax of suffering.

Just so, it is the same for the clean of heart who are made clean only at the price of painful self-uncluttering. And with the peacemakers who must painfully labor to build and to make. But the full meaning of crowned suffering is revealed at the end. "Blessed are they who suffer persecution for justice' sake, for theirs is the kingdom of heaven." We might do well to alert ourselves with the very literal etymological translation: "Blessed are they who suffer the follow-through. Theirs is, right now, the kingdom of Heaven."

We see this possession of the kingdom shine out very brilliantly in the martyrs who went singing to their martyrdoms. We remember St. Thomas More making jest with his executioner on the very scaffold. We recall St. Perpetua arranging her hair becomingly in preparation for being gored by a wild cow. There is Bl. Margaret Clitherow, who spent her last days in an Elizabethan prison making herself a new white dress to wear for her martyrdom. For the lesser lights of sanctity we are, there is also a certain notification given of the possession of the kingdom in the small follow-throughs of daily living in aspiration of sanctity.

We tend to think of persecution as something striking us from without. Often enough it is just that. There is the real persecution suffered by the martyr submitted to torture or sentenced to death for his faith or some doctrine of faith. There are the lesser in vital effect (or maybe we should say vital termination) but not necessarily lesser in intensity persecutions suffered by those who for the sake of their convictions and principles are condemned by the press and other forms of the media. The patient are persecuted by the naggers, the gentle by the aggressive, the weak by the bullies. And then there is the imaginary persecution from without, the technical or amateur paranoid whose imagination creates persecutions out of the blandest normalcies. But there is another persecution. And it comes from within. Everyone aspiring to holiness has got to suffer this follow-through. Let's take a few examples.

"Of courtesy," observes Hilaire Belloc, "It is much less/ than courage of heart or holiness;/ Yet in my walks it seems to me/ that the grace of God is in courtesy."[8] The flowering of this delicate and so endearing natural virtue is not realized without suffering nature's persecution. It does not "come natural" to be courteous with the bore, the curious, the dull. It is a great fallacy to suppose that the exquisite courtesy of Christ toward just those categories of persons

[8]   Hilaire Belloc, "Courtesy."

so conspicuous in the Gospels never suffered persecution. That our blessed Lord was like us in all things save sin includes His being like us temptable. It does no honor to the perfect humanity of Christ to suppose that He never felt frustrated, bored, annoyed. The Gospels show Him weary in body. "Jesus therefore being wearied with his journey, sat thus on the well" (John 4:6). They also show Him weary in soul. "Have I been so long a time with you; and have you not known me?" (John 14:9). His courtesy suffered the persecution of contradiction, stupidity, coarseness and crudeness, insensitivity, and ingratitude. Then, there is patience. St. Paul, who had a bit of trouble in this area, has some observations to make in his second letter to the Corinthians, chapters 11–12. An unpersecuted patience is less patience than a kind of psychological bovineness. The Scriptures make it abundantly clear that patience is a victory won out of suffering and endurance. Victory. Yes, it seems, then, that the patient man was on the battlefield. One opts for patience, but one has to suffer the follow-through if the option is to be secured. There must be the persecution of anger, annoyance, disappointment, aggravation.

For the vowed religious, too, there is a very definite follow-through on each vow in order to attain the holiness to which the vow is a specific means. There is the vocation, the call which can come only from God. And there is the human response, which can come only from the person called. We are always at liberty to say no to God, but it is a sorry sort of liberty to exercise. The realest liberty is to be so free in God that one can no longer be constrained to refuse any of His summons.

We see the rich young man in the Gospel about whose vocation there is no possible doubt. Christ in His physical human presence stood before the boy, loved him, called him. "If thou wilt be perfect, go sell what thou hast, and thou shalt have treasure in Heaven: and come follow me" (Matt. 19:21). The wealthy young fellow chose not to respond. He measured what Jesus asked on his own worldly scales, and the needle pointed to: "Too much." But even for the many who do respond and leave whatever is the equivalent of their fishing nets and boats or their own gold to follow Jesus, there remains a lifelong follow-through.

One who makes a vow of virginal chastity has to suffer in some measure or other persecution by the legitimate demands of nature if she is to realize the fullness of her surrender to Christ. The nun who rises every midnight to pray is not trying to find the most difficult possible time to pray and then set that up as a kind of torturing hazard. No, she breaks her sleep to worship God because this choral worship must be offered by day and by night. So supreme in her life is the call to communal worship of God that the call to sunder her sleep is a clear and obvious one. So it is a spiritual call to which she responds, not some kind of hazards-course training. Still, she will have to suffer persecution from nature to achieve this fullness of response. Weariness and heaviness are the follow-through to be suffered by one who is pledged to offer worship to God by day and by night.

Again, it would be a strange land of fasting where legitimate desires never suffered anything at all. Our blessed Lord in His perfect human nature had even so to suffer persecution from His humanness. We see Him at the very beginning of His public life suffering the persecution of His own body, which would have liked Him to work a miracle to satisfy its very legitimate needs. What the devil suggested, "Command that these stones be made bread" (Matt. 4:3), could not have been a temptation if it were not inviting. "He was hungry" (Matt. 4:2). Christ's hungering body said, "I want to be satisfied." The suggestion of using His miraculous powers to satisfy this legitimate need had to be suffered as a persecution. Back, then, to the vow of religious chastity to whose perfection the curtailment of sleep and fasting have something to contribute. The body has to be gently persuaded by a given heart and a virginal mind to what it is not of itself inclined to do. It has to be lovingly educated by the mind and heart to suffer having its quite legitimate demands go unhonored. Unless the mind is virginal, unless the heart is fully pledged, how shall the body ever be persuaded to consecrated virginity? The mind and heart must lead the body to a height beyond its own comprehension, and they achieve this only in the follow-through of suffering.

So, too, one must suffer persecution for obedience's sake. We may want to recall here once again that "justice" in the scriptural sense is holiness. We suffer for holiness's sake. We see Jesus in the Garden of Gethsemane suffering the persecution of His own human will, which did not want to submit to the Passion, which agonized in its human demand that this should not be, and whose anguish could be superseded only by a greater willing—submission to the will of the Father. If Christ in His perfect human nature had to suffer persecution from His own perfect will so that it be brought into alignment with the will of His Father, it is altogether right and fitting that one vowing obedience should suffer persecution for the alignment of her will with God's. One must suffer the demands of one's own will, which often enough militate against the will of God. One has to agonize sometimes under the persecution of one's own willfulness. If we lovingly dismember that word, willfulness, it becomes rather clear that one cannot become full of the will of God without having suffered the persecution of one's own willfulness. And the stronger the will, and even the willfulness, so much the greater the capacity to be filled with the will of God once one has suffered the follow-through of pledging oneself forever to God in obedience. No one arrives at the perfect liberty that a vow of obedience is meant to make possible and to equip us to experience without having suffered much from many thralldoms. In fact, it is only by suffering the persecution of one's own demanding will, demands which can be put down only by love, that one can be free.

Again, in the vow of poverty, there is persecution to be undergone, a long follow-through. We need to suffer the persecuting demands of our own acquisitiveness not only on the material plane but more especially as regards those far more pressing demands for proprietorship that lie within ourselves. There is the acquisitiveness for excuses, for one thing. There are the demands of our nature for holdings of its own. To surrender all interior acquisitiveness, to give up the last parcel of land on which our own name is written so that we have nothing at all to stand on except God, and to have no holdings at all except the Beloved, requires the strength achieved only in suffering the follow-through of the vow.

The heart makes demands; the body makes demands; mediocrity makes demands; wandering thoughts make demands. What is needed is to suffer all this persecution gladly. One could make example or take example from any virtue or any vow. Each has its follow-through of suffering to arrive us at holiness.

And so Christ looked at His audience on that hillside, some enthralled, some doubtless puzzled; the comprehending and half-comprehending and non-comprehending. He was giving the shortest and most complete of spiritual seminars, offering a blueprint for living whose accuracy is as astonishingly fresh today in the secret chamber or on the six-lane highway as it was on the Mount of the Beatitudes.

We want to be happy. We ache for blessedness, despite all our unblessed behavior. And still the call at once imperious and free goes out: Be poor, be meek, mourn in a true response to penancing truth, hunger and thirst for the justice that begins with your own inner rectitude, be merciful, be pure of heart, make peace. And suffer willingly persecutions without which none of those states of blessedness can be realized. In the end, learn to suffer them gladly. For this is the culmination of blessedness: to suffer the vital follow-through for justice' sake. And you are established, even now, in the kingdom of Heaven.

About the Author

On Valentine's Day 1921, a child was born in Saint Louis, Missouri, to John Aschmann and his forty-seven-year-old wife, Anne Maher Aschmann. The blend of German father and Irish mother would provide felicitous personality traits for their offspring in her future vocation as Mother Abbess. Anne herself baptized the child, due to dire predictions of the doctor that she would not live beyond a fortnight, which happily proved false. She was given the name Alberta in honor of her father's favorite sister. Taught by the School Sisters of Notre Dame, she knew at the age of sixteen that she had to be a sister; and she became a candidate in their motherhouse at Ripa after high school graduation. She attended Saint Louis University, but her time there came to an end just short of attaining her degree.

God's call had sounded in her heart once again, and she knew she had to leave all that was dear to her and become a cloistered contemplative nun. Despite the opposition of her family and almost everyone she knew, Alberta left on July 7, 1942, for Chicago, where she entered the Poor Clare Monastery. A year later, on June 26, she received the holy habit and her new religious name: Sister Mary Francis of Our Lady. Even as a novice, she was permitted by the abbess, Mother Immaculata, to develop her gift of writing poetry, and a first volume, *Whom I Have Loved*, was published while she was still in the novitiate. This work brought her visits by the famous poet and president of Saint Mary's College at Notre Dame, Sister Madeleva, as well as the well-known poet Sister Maura, S.S.N.D., and the daughter of Hilaire Belloc, Eleanor Belloc Jebb, who had been sent by her father to meet this rising literary star.

A year after Sister Francis made final profession on July 26, 1947, Mother Immaculata chose her to be part of the band who would go to unknown Roswell, New Mexico, on November 1, 1948, to make a new Poor Clare foundation. Less than a decade later, the young Sister Francis was commissioned by her abbess to enter a contest for a book written by an unknown author. When Sister inquired what the book should be about, Mother Immaculata replied, "I don't care, just win the prize. The roof needs to be fixed." Sister Francis decided to write about the only thing she knew well, the Poor Clare life, and told the story of the Roswell foundation in *A Right to Be Merry*. The book never made it to the contest because the author's aunt showed the first chapter to her dinner guest, Frank Sheed, who said, "Get me the rest of that book, and I'll publish it." But the roof did get fixed, since the book became the best seller of 1956. Ignatius Press recently published a new edition of this enduring classic.

Other books followed, despite the fact that the author lived a busy Poor Clare life as secretary, organist, portress, librarian, Latin and music teacher, and the sister in charge of the fruit. Many of her poems were written on the backs of fruit labels carefully removed from cans to save paper since the community was very poor. Sister Francis would go out to mow her lawn (with a push mower!) and come up to her cell to write a few lines of the play she was working on about Our Lady of Guadalupe, *Counted as Mine*, or some other book. She claimed that her books just "wrote themselves," but other Poor Clares are still waiting for this to happen! Most demanding of her very limited time was the intense study of manuscripts in medieval French sent to her by monasteries abroad to research the life of

St. Colette for the book *Walled in Light*, published in 1959. These years also saw the writing of several delightful plays, plus another volume of poetry.

On May 19, 1964, the community chose her as its new abbess. The next year, Mother Francis was elected head of the recently formed federation of Colettine Poor Clare monasteries in the United States and began making triennial visitations of the eleven communities scattered throughout the country. Mother served as federal abbess for sixteen years and as federal councilor for thirteen years. She guided the federation through the stormy post-conciliar years, writing a new text of Constitutions, definitively approved in 1981, which has been taken up by monasteries all over the world. Through numerous articles and a vast correspondence, she encouraged religious on every continent to stand firm in preserving the ideals of religious life that were threatened by too-sweeping changes after the Council. Her daughters are especially grateful for her wisdom in retaining the traditional Poor Clare habit, which is a cherished symbol of consecration to this day. Her book *Marginals*, published in 1967, is a commentary on the Vatican II document *Perfectae Caritatis* and gives valuable guidelines for genuine renewal of religious life. Several other of her books were published in the 1960s.

About the Author

In 1972, God's call once again sounded in a dramatic way, as the community in Roswell was asked to make its first foundation in Newport News, Virginia. The vocations that had been drawn to Roswell by the charming little book *A Right to Be Merry* were sent far and wide to spread the ideal of St. Clare. Foundations followed in Alexandria, Virginia (1977), Los Altos Hills, California (1981), Belleville, Illinois (1986), The Netherlands (1990), and Chicago, Illinois (2000). The story of the foundations is told in Mother's own inimitable style in *Forth and Abroad*, published by Ignatius Press in 1997. During these years two more volumes of poetry were published, plus several more books. Mother also made a new translation from the Latin of the Rule of St. Clare and her four extant letters, as well as a translation from the French of the Testament of St. Colette.

In 2002, Mother was honored with the *Pro Fidelitate et Virtute* Award by the Institute on Religious Life for her contributions to consecrated life by her books, her poetry, and her life of contemplative prayer. In 2004, she celebrated her fortieth anniversary as abbess of the Roswell community and the sixtieth anniversary of her religious profession. Her sisters in cloisters throughout the nation and all over the world rise up and call her blessed, giving thanks for the inestimable graces they have received through her inspiring life of outpoured love for Christ, her Lord and Spouse. He came for His faithful bride at 2:35 p.m. on February 11, the feast of Our Lady of Lourdes, with her spiritual daughters gathered around her. Most Rev. Ricardo Ramirez, C.S.B., Bishop of Las Cruces, celebrated the Mass of Christian Burial at 8:30 a.m. on Tuesday, February 14, her eighty-fifth birthday.

Sophia Institute

Sophia Institute is a nonprofit institution that seeks to nurture the spiritual, moral, and cultural life of souls and to spread the Gospel of Christ in conformity with the authentic teachings of the Roman Catholic Church.

Sophia Institute Press fulfills this mission by offering translations, reprints, and new publications that afford readers a rich source of the enduring wisdom of mankind.

Sophia Institute also operates the popular online Catholic resource CatholicExchange.com. *Catholic Exchange* provides world news from a Catholic perspective as well as daily devotionals and articles that will help readers to grow in holiness and live a life consistent with the teachings of the Church.

In 2013, Sophia Institute launched Sophia Institute for Teachers to renew and rebuild Catholic culture through service to Catholic education. With the goal of nurturing the spiritual, moral, and cultural life of souls, and an abiding respect for the role and work of teachers, we strive to provide materials and programs that are at once enlightening to the mind and ennobling to the heart; faithful and complete, as well as useful and practical.

Sophia Institute gratefully recognizes the Solidarity Association for preserving and encouraging the growth of our apostolate over the course of many years. Without their generous and timely support, this book would not be in your hands.

www.SophiaInstitute.com
www.CatholicExchange.com
www.SophiaInstituteforTeachers.org

Sophia Institute Press® is a registered trademark of Sophia Institute.
Sophia Institute is a tax-exempt institution as defined by the
Internal Revenue Code, Section 501(c)(3). Tax I.D. 22-2548708.